Sharks in Danger:
Global Shark Conservation Status with Reference to Management Plans and Legislation

Sharks in Danger: Global Shark Conservation Status with Reference to Management Plans and Legislation

Rachel Cunningham-Day

Universal Publishers
USA – 2001

*Sharks in Danger: Global Shark Conservation Status
with Reference to Management Plans and Legislation*

Copyright © 2001 Rachel Cunningham-Day
All rights reserved.

published by
Universal Publishers / uPUBLISH.com
Parkland, FL USA – 2001

ISBN: 1-58112-652-2

www.upublish.com/books/day.htm

CONTENTS

1.0	Abstract	9
2.0	Introduction	11
3.0	What is a shark?	13
4.0	Why should we be concerned about shark conservation?	15
5.0	Why are sharks in need of protection?	19
6.0	What do we need to know about sharks in order to conserve them?	49
7.0	Fisheries management	57
8.0	Shark conservation bodies	59
9.0	Legislation	67
10.0	International species protection	91
11.0	Detailed case studies of the basking shark (*Cetorhinus maximus*) and the great white shark (*Carcharodon carcharias*)	101
12.0	Conclusions	129

ANNEXES   135

Annex 1	Scientific nomenclature for shark species	135
Annex 2	Fishing methods	139
Annex 3	Fishery bodies	141
Annex 4	Useful web site addresses	149

REFERENCES   151

ACKNOWLEDGEMENTS   201

APPENDICES   203

Appendix 1: Legislation that protects white sharks or identifies their status as needing particular conservation action in Australia   203

Appendix 2: Australia's Grey Nurse Shark Draft Recovery Plan   207

Appendix 3: Australia's Great White Shark Draft Recovery Plan   211

Appendix 4: Draft Discussion Paper Pursuant to CITES Resolution Conf. 9.17   215

Appendix 5: Aims of a National Shark-Plan, as set out in the FAO International Plan of Action for Sharks   219

Appendix 6: IUCN Guidelines for Protected Area Management   221

Appendix 7: Goals of the National Representative System of Marine Protected Areas in Australia   225

TABLES

Table 5.11	Shark uses	20
Table 5.111	Top exporters and importers of shark fins in 1990	22
Table 5.21	Fisheries where collapses have occurred	25
Table 5.221	Estimated large coastal shark commercial landings (lbs) in the Atlantic Ocean and Gulf of Mexico by species	31
Table 5.222	Estimated pelagic shark commercial landings (lbs) in the Atlantic Ocean by species	33
Table 5.223	Estimated small coastal shark commercial landings (lbs) in the Atlantic Ocean by species	33
Table 5.224	Pacific shark landings, by state and coastwide, 1984-99, organized by species group (thousands of lbs)	35
Table 5.31	US commercial and recreational shark landings between 1980 and 1989	40
Table 5.32	Estimated recreational shark harvests (numbers of fish) in the Atlantic Ocean and Gulf of Mexico by subgroup and species	41
Table 8.11	Structure of the Red List categories showing decreasing threatened status	61
Table 8.12	Sharks on the 2000 Red List	62
Table 10.11	CITES Appendices	95
Table 10.12	CITES 2000 Shark Proposals at the 11th Conference of the Parties	98
Table 11.1	Centres of abundance for great white sharks and basking sharks	101
Table 11.1641	Commercial basking shark catches (numbers) 1947-1975	114
Table 11.261	Recreational catch rate data for white sharks in S.E. Australia	123

Global Shark Conservation Status with Reference to Management Plans and Legislation

1.0 ABSTRACT

This book reviews the current status of, and threats to, shark populations globally with special reference to the basking shark and the great white shark. Sharks are a valuable resource both directly through shark watching trips, medical research and commercial and recreational fisheries, and indirectly through the selection pressure they exert on our teleost fisheries, the part they play in maintaining the ecology of the ocean and their intrinsic scientific value. Identifiable threats to sharks are recreational and commercial overfishing and environmental degradation rendered by man, such as development of nursery and mating zones and disturbance of the marine environment through netting and trawling. Particular threats to sharks worldwide are the exploitative fin and cartilage trades. Information required for the sustainable management of sharks includes: life history episodes such as reproductive rates, vulnerable life stages, population dynamics and spatial and temporal distribution. An in depth analysis of white sharks and basking sharks reveals similarities in their reproductive strategies such that similar management practices can be applied to both species. In reviewing fishery management practises it was found that sustainable management plans must be based upon reproductive rates and this requires knowledge of life histories. Life history information is also often required for legislative protection and this means that extremely rare species cannot be considered. Protective legislation should be targeted towards individual species and vulnerable life stages, particularly nursery and mating zones. Further legislation should be enacted to improve current knowledge through required data collection.

2.0 INTRODUCTION

Many shark populations are in danger of extinction as a direct result of man's activities. Sharks are generally hated and feared in the Western world but in Malaita in the Solomon Islands people have worshipped sharks as gods for centuries. However, today the lure of high prices for shark fins has created a market even in some of the Solomon Islands (Sant & Hayes 1996). Management to prevent further destruction and to replenish numbers requires a change in attitudes and an elucidation of shark requirements to enable sustainable trade, fishery and sport activity.

This book will outline why sharks are a valuable resource, identify threats to sharks and where they occur and review what we need to know about sharks in order to protect them. Fisheries management procedures are investigated to target areas requiring future research and implementation. Conservation initiatives, legislation, and international agreements are reviewed and future measures suggested. Case histories on the basking shark and the great white shark detail threats specific to these species and identify research and management requirements. For brevity, scientific nomenclature is contained in Annex 1.

3.0 WHAT IS A SHARK?

The Chondrichthyes possess a distinctive cartilaginous skeleton with bone deposits in teeth and parts of the spine and comprise the sharks, chimaerans, rays, skates and sawfishes. Sharks are distinct from the other Chondrichthyes as they have cylindrical forms, (with the exception of the Squatiniformes), with five to seven gill openings on each side of the head.

There are at least 370 shark species worldwide spanning many ecological types (Hall, 1993:3). Sizes range from the whale shark (13.7m maximum measured length) to the 15-18cm dwarf dogfish. Habitats range from the ocean surface to its depths and, in the case of the bull shark and the Ganges shark, freshwater rivers (Stevens 1987:37). Feeding habits range from the filter feeding basking shark to the apex predator tiger shark and activity levels range from the constantly swimming mako species to the bottom lying nurse shark.

4.0 WHY SHOULD WE BE CONCERNED ABOUT SHARK CONSERVATION?

Published data from the Food and Agriculture Organisation of the United Nations (FAO) show that shark catches have been rising steadily since the 1940s (Anon, 1999d). Today drift gill nets alone kill 3,000 sharks daily (Marine Conservation Society leaflet, 2000). Most sharks are K selected: they have large body size, few natural predators, slow rates of growth, late onset of maturity and small numbers of well-developed young so cannot withstand high levels of predation (Gruber, 1990:188).

4.1 Ocean Ecology and Fisheries

Sharks maintain diversity by preventing explosions of single species. An increase in stingrays and jellyfish along the Florida Panhandle has been attributed to decreasing shark numbers. Shark overfishing in Tasmania caused a boom in their main prey, octopus, which crashed the spiny lobster fishery. Predatory sharks assist their prey's evolution by removing diseased and genetically defective individuals which creates a stable, quality fishery supply. Sharks are distributed worldwide such that the impact of their decline will be widespread.

4.2 Important Economic Resource

Sharks play an important role in the economy through directed commercial and recreational fisheries, the control they exert over other fisheries, trade in shark by-products and ecotourism. In 1993 shark diving in the Maldives was estimated to generate $2.3 million per year such that a grey reef shark was worth one hundred times more alive at a dive site than dead on a fishing boat (Anderson and Ahmed, 1993).

4.3 Medical Research

Sharks may further our medical knowledge if we can explain how:

- shark wounds heal within 24 hours without treatment,
- lacerated corneas remain clear, functional and heal rapidly when blindness follows in other species, and
- sharks resist our attempts to induce cancer tumours.

Scientists recently isolated squalamine, an antibiotic effective against bacteria, fungi and protozoa, from dogfish shark liver oil. A cancer tumour growth requires blood vessels to grow towards it in a process called angiogenesis. Squalamine is an angiogenesis inhibitor and has slowed the growth of brain tumours in rats. It is currently in Phase I clinical trials at the University of Texas (San Antonio) and Georgetown Cancer Center, Washington DC (Anon, 2000f).

4.4 Intrinsic Scientific Value

Sharks exhibit many unique life history traits and behaviours. Predatory sharks can detect blood in very high dilutions and the bull and Ganges sharks are able to osmoregulate in both freshwater and marine environments. Navigation is thought to be in response to magnetic and electrical fields, lunar movements, chemical stimuli and geographical topography. Reproduction includes unique forms of nourishment including interuterine cannabalism in the sand tiger shark. Shark physiology and behaviour, such as attack, mating, schooling and use of nursery grounds, are not fully understood.

5.0 WHY ARE SHARKS IN NEED OF PROTECTION?

Shark numbers are depleting through overfishing, fisheries by-catch, destruction of nursery and mating habitats and increased demand for shark products and aquarium species. Countries attract tourists by promoting shark watching activities, unrestricted sport fishing and using anti-shark measures to decrease the possibility of attack. This has led to severe population depletion in some areas. For example, there are concerns that the nurse shark population in New South Wales is failing to find mates due to low numbers (Anon, 2000b).

5.1 Shark Products

Fisheries are overfishing stocks for a variety of products and uses (see Table 5.11). The FAO reports a doubling of world shark exports between 1985 and 1994. Imports to the EU increased from 27,100 million tonnes (mt) in 1980 to 42,000mt in 1994. An estimated 30 per cent of fish and chip shops in southern England serve "rock salmon" (piked dogfish) which requires imports from the USA and Canada to meet demand (WWF 2000).

Table 5.11 Shark uses

sharks	laboratory animals, commercial and domestic aquaria
fins	soup, traditional medicine
jaws and teeth	jewellery, curios
skin	leather, abrasives
entrails	fishmeal
flesh	food, fertilizer
liver	oil - vitamins, haemorrhoid medicine, paint base squalene - cosmetics, pharmaceuticals, perfumery, lubricate fine mechanisms such as aircraft hydraulic systems and electronics
cartilage	burn treatment (Chondroiten - artificial skin) and biochemicals
blood	anticoagulants
eye	corneal implants

Source: Gruber, 1990:115-121.

The shark fin and cartilage industries currently pose the biggest threats to shark populations.

5.11 Shark Fin Industry

Since the second century BC Asian countries have used fin cartilage in shark fin soup. Today shark fin soup is available worldwide through Asian restaurants and food shops. Shark fin soup fetches upwards of $50 a bowl (Russell, 1996:104) and is considered a powerful aphrodisiac.

More than 150 countries trade in shark fin. Hong Kong Customs data show total imports of shark fins rose from 2.7 million kilos in 1980 to 6.1 million in 1995. However, re-exports are not recorded and Hong Kong often exports raw fins to China which are returned after processing for re-export. Hong Kong dealers note that Japan and Spain are major suppliers of blue shark fins, the Philippines and the Middle East of blacktip reef shark fins, Mexico of hammerhead fins and Mexico, Brazil, the Philippines and Venezuela of oceanic whitetip and tiger shark fins (Parry-Jones 1996). Fins from piked dogfish and porbeagle are exported to Asian countries from Norway, Germany and the UK (Traffic 1997). Retail prices in Hong Kong range from US$40 to $564 per kilo (WWF 2000). The value of fins vary according to species, fin type, condition and regional preference. The lower caudal fin is the most valuable owing to its high fin needle content. Fins from larger sharks are sold as fin sets consisting of the first dorsal, pectoral, and lower caudal fins. Value increases with rarity such that fishermen will expend increasing effort on dwindling populations.

Table 5.111 Top exporters and importers of shark fins in 1990

Exporters	Quantity (million tons)	Importers	Quantity (million tons)
Hong Kong	1,609	Hong Kong	3,838
China	809	China	1,335
Singapore	806	Singapore	1,006
Indonesia	558	USA	192
Japan	451	Malaysia	92
Others	1,172	Others	143

Source: FAO Fisheries Statistics (1994:16)

Shark fins are harvested as a highly lucrative by-catch with little directed effort and storage problems. Shark meat has a low value due to its high urea content. Fishermen utilise their refrigerators for more valuable catch and discard the shark once the fins have been cut off. The high value of shark fins has led to the launch of thousands of directed shark fin longlining vessels with Taiwanese, Japanese, South African and Spanish operators extending from Morocco to Ghana (Cook, 1990:6).

From 1991 to 1998 the number of sharks killed solely for their fins in waters off Hawaii increased by 2500%. On 22 June 2000 a state bill was passed to prohibit the landing of any shark fins in the state of Hawaii unless the shark is landed whole. Similar legislation should be enacted in fisheries where sharks are targeted, or incidentally taken, to reduce this practice and enable catch to be monitored for fisheries management. The shark fin market has expanded rapidly and research is needed to determine the exploitation levels of various species and to assess appropriate conservation measures.

5.12 Shark Cartilage Industry

In 1996 shark cartilage was a $50 million a year industry with between 25-100,000 people using dozens of brands for it's reputed cancer-curing properties (Dold, 1996:53). Today turnover is probably even greater due to supply through high street shops such as Holland & Barrett and increasing usage by European veterinary practices. Cartilage is believed to contain angiogenesis inhibitors. Cartilage can account for up to 6 per cent of shark body weight making them an obvious source for this industry. Twenty seven pounds of shark cartilage produce one pound of extract (Russell,1996:104). One US owned cartilage-extracting plant in Puntarenas, Costa Rica (Corporacion Procesadora Cartilago, SA) exported 131,275kg of cartilage chips between 1 August 1994 (opening of plant) and 30 September 1995. Ninety percent was shipped to US and European markets where capsules sell for over $40 per 100 pills (Russell,1996:104). It is estimated that at least 235,000 large coastal sharks are being processed each month at this plant (Dold, 1996). Four other plants in Puntarenas also process cartilage. As sharks are becoming more scarce Costa Rican fishermen are fishing off Guatemala and illegally fishing in the Galapagos Marine Reserve (Russell,1996:104). Cartilage production is not restricted to Costa Rica. The New Zealand seafood exporters directory lists 2 companies exporting shark cartilage to the US (Sant & Hayes 1996).

The Journal of Clinical Oncology November 1998 contains the results of a three month study conducted by the Cancer Treatment Research Foundation in Illinois on terminally ill cancer patients which concluded that shark cartilage neither slowed the disease nor improved quality of life.

5.2 Overfishing: Commercial and Incidental

It is important to note that most commercial, incidental and recreational shark catches are unregulated and unmonitored such that available data does not represent a true indication of worldwide landings. (See Annex 2 for explanation of fishery methods).

Virtually all major targeted shark fisheries studied have crashed after 3-5 years (Anon, 1995c). Few regulations exist due to lack of catch data and insufficient research funding which are both necessary for the development of management plans. Similar shark species command similar prices so fishermen manage multiple shark species as one generic stock. A species can become severely depleted before the fishery is aware of its condition.

Sharks are caught as incidental by-catch in virtually every commercial fishery and are rarely released. They are generally killed either for their economic value, to avoid the dangers of handling a live shark or because it is impractical to release them from a large catch. Greenpeace Australia calculated that in 1988 alone Taiwanese and Korean squid fleets killed over 2.25 million blue sharks in the north Pacific (Dayton, 1991:34-37). Increases in vessel numbers and capability have increased global pressure. China's distant-water fleet has rapidly expanded from 1 vessel in 1976 to 64 vessels in 1996 in the North Pacific, Atlantic and Indian Oceans (Rose, 1996).

Table 5.21 Fisheries where collapses have occurred

Porbeagle fisheries in the Northwest Atlantic (1968-1972)
California Soupfin Shark Fishery (1930-1944)
Australian School Shark Fishery (1927-1956)
Scottish-Norwegian Spiny Dogfish Fishery (1946 - 1986)
British Columbia Spiny Dogfish Fishery (1907-1949)
Basking Shark Fisheries off Northeast Atlantic and Eastern and Western Pacific
Source: Anderson, 1990:473-474

Fisheries are the single biggest activity to impact upon shark numbers so some countries will be considered further. Fisheries legislation is considered in sections 9 and 10.

5.21 European Fisheries

Landings of sharks in the Northeast Atlantic declined rapidly in the mid 1980s. The small spotted catshark, porbeagle, blue shark, piked dogfish, shortfin mako, and tope are all exploited. Piked dogfish catch declined from 43,411mt in 1987 to 19,621mt in 1994.

Mediterranean shark landings averaged 21,000mt annually from 1980 to 1993. The main shark species landed are the small spotted catshark, piked dogfish, smooth-hound, longnose spurdog, blackmouth catshark, gulper sharks, bluntnose sixgill shark, blue shark, shortfin mako and thresher shark.

5.211 UK Fisheries

Large numbers of sharks are taken by commercial and recreational fisheries around the British Isles. The limited quantitative data available for landings and effort show evidence of decreasing catches (Vas, 1995).

Vas (1995:73) defined British sharks as being either:

1) Exploited - species targeted specifically by either recreational or commercial fisheries. Plus any species landed in large numbers, i.e. > 500 sharks per year.

2) By-catch - species regularly taken as incidental catches in fisheries directed at other species. Plus species landed in small numbers, i.e. < 500 sharks per year.

3) Non-exploited - any species which is not taken regularly by either commercial or recreational fisheries. Such species are represented in catches by < 5 individuals per year.

Of the 21 species of shark found in British waters, 6 are exploited, 4 are by-catch (angelshark, thresher, smoothhound, starry smoothound), and 11 non-exploited. By-catch from the Spanish swordfish fishery in the north-east Atlantic off the North and North West coasts of Spain takes a large by-catch of pelagic sharks which may reduce the number of sharks reaching British waters, highlighting the need for international management of shark stocks.

Blue Sharks - EXPLOITED - taken by recreational fisheries in England and Ireland. Since 1991 blue sharks have also been targeted by an unregulated small-scale longline fishery off the southern coast of Cornwall which exports sharks to France (Mitchell, 1991:81-82).

Recreational catches of blue shark have decreased in the western English Channel and in Cornwall with declining Catch Per Unit Effort (CPUE) suggesting commercial overfishing (Vas, 1990, 1994). The Shark Angling Club of Great Britain record catches of over 6000 sharks in 1960-61 decreasing to fewer than 125 sharks in 1986. 85-90% of the UK blue shark catch are female and caught just as they are about to breed for the first time, highlighting the need for fisheries to regulate catch according to sex, size and season (Anon 1995c).

Porbeagle - EXPLOITED - taken as incidental by-catches in Welsh and English fisheries and in a directed fishery in the Bristol channel where catch rates can reach 4 fish per day up to a weight of 125kg per individual (Dulvy, pers.comm.). A small scale directed longline fishery has operated off the Shetland Islands since 1987. France, Norway and Denmark have directed longline fisheries in British waters. Porbeagles are targeted by recreational fisheries at Aberystwyth and Swansea Bay in Wales, Padstow in northern Cornwall and off northeastern England, the Dorset coast and the Irish coast.

Greater spotted dogfish, lesser spotted dogfish, spurdog – EXPLOITED – taken as by-catch, by recreational fisheries and directed fisheries for spurdog. Few are taken by foreign vessels. Recreational fisheries for spurdog in Ireland show evidence of decreasing CPUE

(Anon, 1993b). Of the 18 spurdog fisheries in Great Britain, only 3 are currently increasing, all others having collapsed (Dulvy, pers.comm.) Longline fisheries can catch up to 50 tonnes in 10-12 days so can cause large stock depletions in a short amount of time. The lesser spotted dogfish fishery operates in most crab/lobster potting areas as they are used for pot bait (Dulvy, pers.comm).

Soupfin - EXPLOITED - taken as by-catch and as recreational catch in England and Ireland.

The basking shark used to be exploited but, following declining catch, is now protected in British coastal waters (12 miles out to sea). Norway, the only country in receipt of an EC quota, has not caught basking shark in the past few years.

No directed commercial or recreational fisheries exist for any other shark species in Britain although various species are taken as incidental captures by fisheries throughout the British Isles.

In 1997 and 1998 Vas conducted a survey of fisheries at Newlyn, near Penzance. Spurdog was a direct catch whereas catshark, blue, porbeagle, tope and six-gill sharks were by-catch. All were predominantly caught with longlines and gill nets. The blue shark was the principal shark by-catch from this inshore fishery forming 79% of landings. Blue, porbeagle and shortfin mako were also caught by French and Spanish tuna drift nets in the Bay of Biscay. Drift net fisheries were found to produce the highest mortality upon shark populations.

5.22 US Fisheries

Overfishing in the Atlantic and Pacific caused populations of tuna, sea bass, red snapper and swordfish to dwindle. Fisheries turned to more abundant shark meat such as mako, thresher and blacktip. In the 1980s sharks became commercially important due to a federal marketing campaign and improved methods of handling. Catch soared from 300,000 pounds in 1979 to 15.7 million pounds in 1989 (11 million pounds representing large coastal sharks, a four fold increase from three years earlier) (Manire and Gruber, 1990). Catches declined by 23 percent the following year due to population reduction (Ellis, 1995).

Atlantic dogfish landings increased by 250 percent between 1985 and 1994 (other sharks by almost 300 per cent) (Rose, 1998). Recent Atlantic landings are shown in the tables below:

Table 5.221 Estimated large coastal shark commercial landings (lbs) in the Atlantic Ocean and Gulf of Mexico by species

Species	1997	1998
Bignose	2,132	50
Blacktip	1,506,182	1,893,805
Bull	40,247	27,389
Dusky	80,930	81,124
Hammerhead	79,685	59,802
Lemon	20,595	23,232
Night	33	3,289
Nurse	8,864	2,846
Reef	3,548	100
Sand tiger	8,425	38,791
Sandbar	890,881	1,077,161
Silky	13,920	13,615
Spinner	6,039	16,900
Tiger	6,603	12,174
White	1,315	-------
Large Coastal (unknown)	98,726	172,038
Unclassified (assumed to be large coastal)	1,078,813	1,038,530
Unclassified fins (assumed to be large coastal)	140,638	76,588
Total	3,987,576 (1,809 mt)	4,537,434 (2,058 mt)

Source: Cortes, 1999c.

Table 5.222 Estimated pelagic shark commercial landings (lbs) in the Atlantic Ocean by species

Species	1997	1998
Bigeye thresher	5,308	1,403
Blue	904	706
Shortfin mako	224,362	222,920
Longfin mako	7,867	4,410
Mako, unclassified	71,371	79,773
Oceanic whitetip	2,764	22,049
Porbeagle	4,222	19,795
Thresher	145,253	102,530
Pelagic sharks, unclassified	694	111
Shark, unclassified (assumed pelagic)	74,849	49,502
Total	537,594 (244 mt)	503,199 (228 mt)

Source: Cortes, 1999c.

Table 5.223 Estimated small coastal shark commercial landings (lbs) in the Atlantic Ocean by species

Species	1997	1998
Atlantic sharpnose	256,562	230,920
Blacknose	202,781	119,689
Bonnethead	75,787	13,949
Finetooth	169,733	267,224
Shark, unclassified (assumed small coastal sharks)	51	82
Total	704,914 (320 mt)	631,864 (287 mt)

Source: Cortes, 1999c.

Pacific shark landings between 1985 and 1994 fluctuated around 5,000 metric tons of mainly spiny dogfish but in 1993 1,800mt of pelagic sharks were caught in the Pacific as by-catch in tuna and swordfish fleets relocating from the Atlantic (Rose 1998). In 1998 the five Pacific states landed over 10.4 million pounds of shark (Camhi, 1999). However, data from the Pacific Fisheries Commission (Table 5.224) do not support these findings. It is difficult to ascertain which data set is the more accurate. This highlights the inconsistencies present in both methods of collection and presentation of data. Care must be taken when extrapolating from landing data.

Table 5.224 Pacific shark landings, by state and coastwide, 1985-99, organized by species group (thousands of lbs)

Species Name	85	86	87	88	89	90	91	92	93	94	95	96	97	98	99
Spiny Dogfish	298	116	164	198	291	484	898	1,100	1,270	1,392	367	249	425	462	514
Leopard Shark	29	32	23	18	22	18	21	19	22	9	9	6	11	14	13
Soupfin Shark	133	103	104	67	78	60	50	46	39	55	44	65	63	54	74
Blue Shark	1	2	2	3	6	20	1	1	1	12	5	1	1	3	0
Shortfin Mako	148	310	402	322	255	373	218	142	122	128	95	96	132	98	62
Other Shark	1,135	1,126	861	454	250	235	169	118	73	25	19	17	33	55	54
Thresher Shark	1,282	1,022	583	499	520	389	615	312	320	367	305	340	385	338	320
Unspecified Shark	90	78	81	22	11	9	6	6	5	6	16	5	6	7	13
Total	3116	2789	2220	1583	1433	1588	1978	1744	1852	1994	860	779	1056	1031	1050

Source: PacFIN data base, 05/2000, Pacific States Marine Fisheries Commission, 7600 Sand Pt. Way, NE, Seattle, WA, 98115.Source: Anon, 1999c.

5.23 Australian Fisheries

Japanese tuna longline vessels in Tasmanian waters took an estimated by-catch of 34,000 finned immature or subadult blue and 1,594 shortfin mako sharks annually. Tasmanian waters represent only one area of the Australian Fisheries Zone fished by Japanese longliners (Stevens, 1992:

227-36). Finning is now in contravention of a subsidiary agreement between the Governments of Australia and Japan (Anon 1994e).

5.24 New Zealand Fisheries
Eleven licenses issued for southern bluefin tuna and seven for northern tuna fisheries have been taken by Japanese fleets which are believed to be finning and taking a substantial catch of large pelagic sharks particularly blue and mako sharks (Sant & Hayes 1996).

5.25 Canadian Fisheries
After 35 uninterrupted years of commercial spiny dogfish landings in British Columbia, a 58% catch decline occurred between 1990 and 1993 resulting in no reported landings in 1994. A declining trend in this species has also occurred in Pacific Northwest landings since 1990 suggesting decline in Pacific North American waters may follow (Cook, 1996:13).

5.26 Taiwanese Fisheries
Despite whale sharks recently becoming a delicacy, catch is mainly by harpoon or by-catch in set nets. Due to its high market value, docility and habit of surface swimming harpooning is increasing. The current combined annual catch is estimated to be 272 individuals (158 set net; 114 harpoon). Harpoon fishermen south of Penghu regularly harvested

50-60 individuals each spring. Catch declined to under 10 in 1994 and 1995. Catch effort has probably increased due to demand which indicates population decline, although environmental factors such as prey abundance or water temperature could be relevant. Whale sharks are auctioned at unofficial, unregulated markets to avoid fees. Local markets sell meat for around NT$400 (US$15) per kg (Che-Tsung *et al.*, 1997).

5.27 Mexico Fisheries

Annual catch of 33,500mt occurred between 1982-1993. Unlike developed countries with high discard, all catch is processed for the consumer market. Conservation measures must take account of this dependency. Since 1992 the National Fisheries Institute has sponsored a national research program and a joint research effort with the United States.

5.28 Indian Ocean Fisheries

Ten shark species are believed to be over-exploited (TRAFFIC 2000). Increased efficiency of Southeast Asian fleets has increased catch of migratory species since the 1980s. By September 2000 the UN Straddling Stocks Agreement had 48 parties. India, Madagascar, Malaysia, South Africa and Thailand were notably absent. India's east coast longline shark fisheries occurred in response to declining shrimp catches. A number of Sri Lankan vessels participate illegally in this fishery.

In 1996 Philippine whale shark landings were the lowest recorded in a hunting season. Philippine whale shark hunting practices remain traditional suggesting exploitative external fishing pressures (Trono, 1996:13). In Thailand, Cristian Mietz spotted 44 whale sharks in 1998, 15 in 1999 and 8 in 2000. Whale shark fisheries are operating in Indonesia, India (on the coast of Gujarat) and Malaysia with illegal harvesting and export in the Philippines (Anon 2000g).

5.29 Turkish Fisheries
Spiny dogfish and smooth hound are targeted in the Black Sea and smooth hounds and lesser spotted dogfish in the northern Aegean. The commercial swordfish longline fishery in the Gulf of Antalya takes thresher sharks incidentally. Purse seine vessels land bluntnose sixgill shark in the Sea of Marmara. No shark management measures are implemented. Smooth hound take has decreased from 5,140mt in 1989 to 2,880mt in 1994. Factors contributing to this reduction have not been investigated (Kabasakal, 1998).

For further information on fisheries see Rose 1996 and Sant & Hayes 1996.

5.3 Overfishing: Recreational Fisheries

Data from Florida shark tournaments from 1970 covering 34 locations, show a 50% drop in shark catches between 1986 and 1989 (Heuter, 1992). A trend can be observed that commercial landings increased whilst recreational landings decreased. Taken with the knowledge that a third of Florida's shark tournaments were abandoned in the mid to late 1980s because sharks were too scarce (Russell, 1996:61) it would suggest that the commercial landings were exploitative, although the data does not take account of effort. Recreational fisheries alone may not be exerting undue pressure on shark populations but in light of current commercial takes they exert further strain on already exploited populations.

Table 5.31 US commercial and recreational shark landings between 1980 and 1989

US Commercial Shark Landings (in metric tons)		U.S. Recreational Shark Landings (in metric tons)	
Year	Landings	Year	Landings
1980	458	1980	3210
1981	666	1981	9431
1982	590	1982	2599
1983	724	1983	5527
1984	846	1984	1975
1985	969	1985	5305
1986	1618	1986	4243
1987	3603	1987	4175
1988	5276	1988	2728
1989	7122	1989	1666

Source: National Marine Fisheries Service (1999b)

Recreational take is regulated in some countries (see section 9 for details) but developing countries attract tourists by advertising unrestricted game fishing. Recreational fisheries target some species more than others. A marked decline occurred in the number and proportion of white sharks in the catch off south eastern Australia since the 1970s. The ratio of white sharks to all species caught changed from 1:22 in the 1960s to 1:38 in the 1970s to 1:651 in the 1980s. (Pepperell, 1992:224). The game fishery off the eastern United States decreased from 1:67 to 1:210 between 1965 and 1983 (Casey and Pratt, 1985:2-14).

Table 5.32 Estimated recreational shark harvests (numbers of fish) in the Atlantic Ocean and Gulf of Mexico by subgroup and species

Subgroup	Species	1997	1998
Large Coastal Sharks	Blacktip	68,284	76,552
	Bull	1,254	802
	Dusky	13,278	4,277
	Hammerhead	618	384
	Hammerhead, great	379	441
	Hammerhead, scalloped	3,320	1,101
	Hammerhead, smooth	2,176	370
	Lemon	2,354	1,992
	Night	90	--
	Nurse	7,859	2,690
	Reef	10	--
	Sandbar	40,929	33,245
	Silky	240	5,039
	Spinner	3,342	7,119
	Tiger	70	1,302
	Unclassified	16,298	16,505
Pelagic Sharks	Blue	4,265	6,003
	Shortfin mako	2,618	5,581
	Thresher	1,436	36
Small Coastal Sharks	Atlantic angel	--	107
	Atlantic sharpnose	65,530	42,048
	Blacknose	10,761	9,578
	Bonnethead	15,730	26,191
	Finetooth	5,000	--

Source: Cortes, 1999; Anon, 1999a.

Sport fishing organisations can play an important role in shark conservation through reporting illegal or unusual practises and collecting data for use in shark management plans. Many tournaments establish minimum sizes for species like shortfin mako and blue sharks, and some tournaments encourage catch and release fishing by offering prize points for released sharks (Anon, 2000). Some groups operate tag and release schemes (eg. The Gulf Coast Shark Census and The Elkhorn Slough 'Rod and Reel' shark contests in the US). However, conventional tagging can cause mortality and other sub lethal effects so is inappropriate for non-robust populations (Skomal and Chase, 1996:8-9, Bruce 1999).

5.4 Protection Measures

Shark netting programmes were adopted in Sydney in 1937 to reduce attacks on swimmers. Subsequent netting occurred in Newcastle, Australia (1950), Natal (1952), Hawaii (1959), Queensland (1963) and Dunedin, New Zealand (1969-70). Drumlines are also used in Queensland and consist of a marker buoy and float anchored to the bottom supporting a trace and baited hook. Beach nets and drumlines intercept and catch sharks on their regular feeding and territorial runs (Eckersley 1996).

Natal Shark Board nets annual catch totals 1,345 large sharks of 14 species of which about 13% are tagged and released (Dudley, 1995:1-2). Nets have a selective impact upon sharks as they pose no barrier to smaller sharks (Dudley et.al., 1993:251-252), bottom dwelling sharks display a higher survival rate when caught in nets than surface or middle depth sharks (Reid and Krogh, 1992:295) and rates of inshore-offshore movements, seasonal and along-shore migration patterns and amounts of time certain species spend inshore affect trends in catch per unit effort (CPUE) (Simpfendorfer, 1993). CPUE trends indicate that the shark meshing programme in North Queenland, Australia, has reduced populations of hammerhead, blacktip and whaler sharks by up to 80% (catches were highest in spring and summer indicating nearshore migrations for pupping and mating) but has had little effect on tiger sharks (Simpfendorfer, 1991). Netting restricts access to nursery and mating areas which impacts heavily upon recruitment rates.

Experiments on the use of electrical fields to repel sharks have been carried out in South Africa since 1965 (Cliff and Dudley 1992) but have encountered many logistical problems (Gribble 1996). All sharks found alive in shark nets should be tagged before release, with a method appropriate to the population's vulnerability (see Section 6.4), to assist with studies of population size, growth rates and migratory movements. All dead sharks should be autopsied for life history information.

5.5 Habitat Degradation

Localised pollution and ecological imbalance are thought to have little effect on marine sharks due to their wide range and variety of prey.

However, trawling and netting can disturb large areas and the effects of these practices have not been quantified. Nursery and mating zones are important for the replenishment of shark populations and these coastal and estuary zones are vulnerable to destruction from human settlement and development. Half of the total human world population lives within 100km of the ocean and an increasing amount of coastline is being developed for an ever-expanding tourist industry. Nearshore decline of smooth hammerheads in central Mediterranean sites has been attributed to development (Anon, 1996f:10), and school sharks have declined due to degradation of seagrass meadows in bays around Tasmania (Olsen, 1984).

Freshwater sharks, the euryhaline bull and obligate freshwater Ganges, inhabit physically restricted environments limiting escape from pollutants, habitat modification and destruction, and capture in fisheries. Short and long term fluctuations in temperature, oxygen level, mineral content, turbidity, water flow, rainfall, and major changes in river and lake beds make freshwater habitats less stable than marine equivalents. Human induced problems such as dam building, irrigation water usage, and pollutants from mining operations, industry, agriculture, sewage and deforestation are escalating. Such practises could be devastating to freshwater elasmobranchs in restricted bodies of water (Compagno and Cook, 1995;4-5) as illustrated by the decline in bull sharks in Lake Nicaragua due to overfishing (Thorson, 1982:2-10) and in the Essequibo River, Guyana, due to a cyanide waste spill (Cook, 1995:10).

5.6 Public Opinion

Public opinion predominantly holds that sharks are man-eaters making shark conservation a low priority and shark fishing a popular activity. In fact, worldwide there are 50-75 shark attacks annually resulting in 5-10 deaths (Burgess, 1990). Eighty per cent of shark species are either ill equipped to hurt people or never encounter people (Anon, 1996a). Most 'shark attacks' should be called 'shark defences' because the shark is defending itself against provocation (Perrin, 1995:13). Unprovoked attacks are extremely rare and the majority seem to occur near pinniped colonies where the shark mistakes the human for it's normal prey (Collier, 1992).

5.7 Dive and Cage Operations

The rise in popularity of scuba diving and cage diving has increased the potential for human damage to the marine environment. There have been reports from Seal Rocks, New South Wales (NSW) of scuba divers disturbing grey sharks (Pollard *et al* 1996). Commercial shark dives often feed sharks. Sharks may begin to associate humans with food. Cage dive operators often attract sharks by releasing a mixture of fish oil and/or animal products into the water at regular time intervals to develop a slick ("berleying"). This practise may effect local prey species such as pinnipeds, particularly in pupping season, and introduce viral or bacterial contamination to the marine environment (Presser & Allen 1995). Baiting has been banned from the Monterey Bay National Marine Sanctuary.

Dive trips offer a good opportunity for data collection and the dive community can be a powerful enforcement tool by reporting suspicious activities. If divers keep their distance from the sharks and do not feed them it is unlikely that scuba diving *per se* has any detrimental effects on the sharks (Otway and Parker 1999a).

Poorly managed scuba and cage dives may deter shark populations from residing in the area. All operators offering cage and shark dives should be licensed and strictly regulated as in South Africa. In South Australia (SA) licensed cage divers must fill out and submit a logbook with details of shark sightings. Divers should not be allowed in areas recognised as vulnerable such as nursery and mating zones. In addition, the tourist trade generated by shark watching activities can be damaging. Gans Bay in South Africa had six cage dive operators in 1998 and this has resulted in illegal landings in order to sell jaws and teeth to the tourists (Anon 1998c). Education must form an integral part of shark watching programmes.

5.8 Aquarium Trade

Heavily depleted shark populations cannot sustain further losses to support the aquarium trade. There are currently 36 grey nurse within commercial aquaria in Australia and their population numbers in the wild are thought to be very low (Anon 2000b). Shark populations must be assessed to ensure they can support the removal of individuals and take must be controlled through licence to ensure vulnerable species are not removed for private aquaria. Sharks in aquaria must be on public display and be presented alongside educational programmes informing the public on the biology, conservation management and status of the species. Captive breeding programmes must be instigated, even if the shark species is not threatened, in order to increase our knowledge of shark life history and behaviour as this may benefit other species.

6.0 WHAT DO WE NEED TO KNOW ABOUT SHARKS IN ORDER TO CONSERVE THEM?

The success of future management directions will depend on a better understanding of the biology and behaviour of each shark species. The life history pattern of a species is the characteristic set of biological episodes and responses occurring during the lifetimes of the individuals in the population (Hoenig and Gruber, 1990:2). Elucidation of age at maturity, brood size and survival rates to adulthood are needed to construct sustainable management plans. The lower the fecundity (reproductive capacity) the more time is required for stock replenishment.

6.1 Reproduction

Shark species display different reproductive strategies with varying fecundity:

Oviparous sharks (Orectolobiformes, Heterodontidae, Scyliorhinidae) deposit eggs on the ocean floor and take several months to hatch depending on the water temperature. Brood size varies with species.
Ovoviviparity involves live birth with the eggs developing within the

sharks body. The piked dogfish produces ten or so young after a gestation period of 22 months.

Viviparity (Squaliformes, Carcharinidae, Sphyrnidae) involves live birth with the young obtaining food from the mother during gestation. Gestation periods are 9-12 months with litters between 2-16, although the sand tiger shark has a litter of one as the first embryo to hatch within the uterus consumes its siblings before feeding on maternal eggs (Gilmore, 1980:65).

Reproductive rate is generally highest for oviparous species and lowest for viviparous species, although species variation within each strategy is such that overlap exists.

Sharks also exhibit different breeding cycles. Some species reproduce throughout the year whilst others have a seasonal cycle. Some species have ova ripening in the ovary whilst embryos are developing so the female is ready to ovulate again after birth. In other sharks only a proportion of the mature females breed each year, the others enter a resting stage for a year or possibly longer.

6.2 Nursery Zones

Most shark species restrict their young to nursery areas separate from the adult population which protects them from cannabalism and reduces competition for food. Nursery areas utilised by several species reduce inter-specific predation as adults tend to remain separate from their own juveniles (Springer, 1967:149-174). Temporal separation of species reduces competition for food in Cleveland Bay, northern Australia, where the whitecheek shark occurs during autumn and winter and the creek whaler and blacktip sharks occur during late spring and summer (Simpfendorfer & Milward, 1993:337).

Known nursery areas include the sheltered bays and estuaries around Tasmania, Australia (tope and gummy sharks) (Williams and Schaap, 1992:237-250), coastal waters and estuaries in northern Australia (whaler and hammerhead sharks) (Simpfendorfer and Milward, 1993:337-345), and nearshore areas within the Mediterranean (smooth hammerhead, dusky, copper and great white sharks). A variety of coastal, pelagic and deepwater species are known to occur in the San Francisco Bay estuary (brown smoothhound, leopard, piked dogfish, spotted sevengill, tope, and bluntnose sixgill sharks) some of which are thought to use the Bay as a nursery area (Anon, 1996f:10). Open coastal areas such as sandy beach flats are important for sharks that feed on benthic invertebrates e.g. houndsharks (Anon, 1996f:10).

Declines in lower trophic levels affect top predator food supply causing both a decline in predator number and forcing juveniles to expand their hunting activities into less protected waters. In Florida, USA lemon sharks have declined due to overfishing and loss of mangroves in nursery areas.

6.3 Mating Zones

All sharks practise internal fertilisation. Matings have been documented in shallow water zones for the whitetip reef shark (Tricas et.al. 1985:233-237) and the nurse shark (Klimley, 1980: 878-883; Pratt et.al. 1995:44-53). Matings may involve group behaviour, as witnessed in the nurse shark (Carrier et.al., 1994: 646-655). Mating zones must be identified and closed to the public during breeding seasons. Dry Tortugas National Park in the Florida Keys closes a nurse shark mating zone from May to August (Carrier, 1996:9).

6.4 Migrations and Population Trends

Many shark species are migratory, moving through national boundaries and exclusive economic zones (EEZ). International cooperation is needed to ensure that protective measures undertaken in one country are not undone in another. Conservation of sharks requires verification of migration and population trends in order to convince other nations to participate in their management.

Most sharks can be categorised as :

1) highly pelagic - ranging over broad geographical areas
2) coastal pelagic - generally confined to continental shelves but have shown movements exceeding 1,000 miles
3) resident - range of a few hundred miles or less.

In 1962 the U.S. Government initiated a volunteer shark tagging and release programme. Maximum straight-line recorded distance for a tagged blue shark (pelagic) is 3,740 miles yet multiple recaptures suggest blue sharks may make round-trip movements between North America and Europe that exceed 10,000 miles (Casey and Kohler, 1990:89).

A variety of fish tagging methods can be used to study migrations and monitor population dynamics. However, capture induced mortality or sublethal stress (eg/ reduced growth, reduced capacity to feed, interrupting reproductive effort or greater chance of attack from other sharks (Bruce 1999)) may be unacceptably high. Capturing sharks in order to tag induces additional stress unacceptable to already vulnerable populations. However, sharks that are incidentally caught or trapped in shark meshing should be tagged before release with a method appropriate to the estimated resilience of the population. Bearing in mind that a conventionally tagged animal must be re-captured to be re-identified the indications are that some populations are not sufficiently robust to withstand the risks associated with such studies. Satellite tracking (unit attaches to the dorsal fin of the restrained shark), internal ultrasonic transmitters and archival tags (attached to free swimming sharks) which record light, depth, water temperature and location every few minutes for up to several years are expensive but very effective research methods which do not require recapture to obtain information. Variables in tracking data are compared to shifts in prey abundance or environmental change such as fishing or pollution.

Sharks generally segregate by size and sex so different segments of the population will have different migration patterns. Sharks may be divided into isolated breeding populations which must be identified, through tagging or genetic studies, to elucidate vulnerable life stages and to determine whether locally-depleted regions can be replenished from other areas. Isolated blue shark breeding populations occur in Australia. In NSW blue sharks birth from October to November

(Stevens, 1984:573-90) whereas off north-western Australia birth occurs between December and March (Stevens and McLoughlin, 1991:151-99).

6.5 Age Structure

Management plans depend on stock assessments that estimate age structure. Growth rate, age at maturity, longevity, and mortality rate provide insight into a species' ability to sustain a fishery. Several methods exist for estimating shark age:

1. plotting the sizes of sharks caught in the fishery and assigning age classes to distribution peaks (bearing in mind that sharks grow slowly once they have matured)

2. shark tagging studies to elucidate age and rates of growth

3. observing the degree of calcification at the edge of the vertebral centra (centrum edge analysis)

4. recording peaks of calcium and phosphorous concentrations in the centra and correlating these with growth rings and

5. counting the number of calcified rings which are deposited in the vertebral centra of the shark as it ages.

Methods 3, 4 and 5 require shark dissection.

7.0 FISHERIES MANAGEMENT

Management plans require knowledge of reproductive capacity in order to ensure a sustainable level of exploitation. Estimates of population dynamics can be achieved through demographic analysis (Caughley, 1977; Jenkins 1988), which requires:

(a) estimates of age-specific mortality and natality rates and

(b) information on the distribution, abundance, habits and reproduction of the population

to produce reliable estimates of population growth and size limits. It is necessary to identify isolated breeding populations so they can be managed as discrete units. This information can be provided by fisheries data, tag and recapture results and genetic studies. Demographic studies have been completed for the spiny dogfish (Jones and Geen, 1977; Wood et al, 1979; Hanchet 1988), the soupfin shark (Grant et al., 1979), the lemon shark (Hoenig & Gruber 1990), the sandbar shark (Hoff, 1990) and the leopard shark (Cailliet, 1992:183-93). Studies should be conducted for all fished shark species.

For sustainable yield to increase, fishing effort must be reduced to less than the rate of recruitment. Allowances must also be made for seasonal variation in the available catch and for the likely high cost of identifying the optimal population size (Campbell et.al., 1992:251-62). Maximum Sustainable Yield (MSY) estimates have been unsuccessful in managing teleost fisheries suggesting habitat and vulnerable life stage protection must also be employed.

Stock assessment of shark fisheries is difficult as catch data often fail to differentiate between species and not all catches are reported. In practice, size limits are rarely employed due to lack of life history information (Cailliet, 1990) and gear that does not allow live release of undersized sharks. Catch limits also require life history information and are difficult to enforce. Closed areas and seasons have been used (Bedford, 1987:161-171; Richards 1987:147-160; Holts 1988:1-8) but mating and nursery zones are not known for most shark species. The Precautionary Principle, namely thoughtful action in advance of scientific proof, must be employed for fisheries as all stock assessments are merely estimates. This may mean closing some fisheries to allow stock replenishment.

8.0 SHARK CONSERVATION BODIES

Some environmental bodies include shark conservation in their agendas. In 1998 the UK Marine Conservation Society played a significant role in listing the basking shark onto the Wildlife and Countryside Act 1981. The Ocean Wildlife Campaign hosted the first International Pelagic Shark Workshop in Honolulu in February 2000. Shark experts from 14 countries presented research results and discussed global shark status including a report from the International Council for the Exploration of the Seas' (ICES) Study Group of Elasmobranch Fishes. The National Audubon Society and SeaWeb inform the public about shark issues through their web sites and publications. WildAid is surveying UK fish and chip shops to ascertain the extent and source of spiny dogfish consumption with the aim of reducing imports from the USA and Canada. TRAFFIC (Trade Records Analysis of Flora and Fauna in Commerce) is the wildlife trade monitoring programme of the World Wide Fund for Nature and the World Conservation Union. It has seven regional programmes most of which have been investigating and reporting on the shark trade. In 1996 WWF International and Unilever PLC/NV created a Marine Stewardship Council to enable consumers to purchase from certified sustainable fisheries. The aim is to unite the efforts of industry and the consumer to promote market-led incentives for sustainable fishing.

Many specific shark conservation initiatives have been formed in recent years. The Shark Trust is the UK member of the European Elasmobranch Association and was set up in 1997 in response to the increasing amount of work relating to sharks being undertaken by English Nature. The Shark Trust collaborates with other bodies to promote elasmobranch conservation and plays an important role in public education. The American Elasmobranch Association achieves similar aims. Peter Benchley (author of "Jaws") currently supports a campaign in Asia to end the finning practice (Chan 2000, Scott 2000). Shark conservation bodies should receive government funding, as fisheries departments, in response to international initiatives, would otherwise undertake their work, and they play leading roles in conserving valuable national resources.

8.1 Red List of Threatened Animals

The United Nations Environment Programme World Conservation Monitoring Centre (UNEP-WCMC) compiles the Red List of Threatened Animals listing species according to threatened status. The list has no legal force but is used by conservation bodies when setting priorities. The Shark Specialist Group (SSG) advises on shark species listings. UNEP-WCMC also issue Guidelines for Protected Area Management Categories which may indirectly assist in the conservation of some shark species (see Appendix 6).

Table 8.11 Structure of the Red List categories showing decreasing threatened status

- Extinct (E)
- Extinct in the Wild (EW)
- Critically Endangered (CR)
- Endangered (EN)
- Vulnerable (VU)
- Lower Risk (LR) either Conservation Dependent (cd), Near Threatened (nt) or Least Concern (lc)
- Data Deficient (DD)
- Not Evaluated (NE)

Source: Anon (1994b:11).

The criteria used to designate categories measures population decline in terms of generations, making it possible to include K-selected species where precise data on population size and declines are not available. One of five criteria needs to be met for a species to qualify for threatened status, and quantitative thresholds apply to define the category of threat. Lack of knowledge of marine ecosystems and their component species hampers the application of criteria. The main evidence for the assessment of sharks is taken from life history knowledge and historical records of former fisheries combined with present-day observations of population levels. Criteria and categories will change from December 2000.

Table 8.12 Sharks on the 2000 Red List

Order: Carcharhiniformes
Family: Carcharhinidae
Graceful shark (*Carcharhinus amblyrhinchoides*) – LR/nt
Grey reef shark (*Carcharhinus amblyrhynchos*) – LR/nt
Pigeye shark / Java shark (*Carcharhinus amboinensis*) - DD
Borneo shark (*Carcharhinus borneensis*) – EN C2b
Spinner shark (*Carcharhinus brevipinna*) – LR/nt
Silky shark (*Carcharhinus falciformis*) – LR/lc
Pondicherry shark (*Carcharhinus hemiodon*) – VU C2a
Smoothtooth blacktip shark (*Carcharhinus leiodon*) - VU B1+2c, C2b
Bull shark (*Carcharhinus leucas*) – LR/nt
Blacktip shark (*Carcharhinus limbatus*) – LR/nt
Oceanic whitetip shark (*Carcharhinus longimanus*) – LR/nt
Blacktip reef shark (*Carcharhinus melanopterus*)- LR/nt
Dusky shark (*Carcharhinus obscurus*) – LR/nt
Sandbar shark (*Carcharhinus plumbeus*) – LR/nt
Tiger shark (*Galeocerdo cuvier*) – LR/nt
Ganges shark (*Glyphis gangeticus*) - CR A1cde+2cde, C2b
Speartooth shark (*Glyphis glyphis*) - EN C2a
Lemon shark (*Negaprion brevirostris*) – LR/nt

Blue shark (*Prionace glauca*) – LR/nt

Atlantic sharpnose shark (*Rhizoprionodon terraenovae*) – LR/lc

Spadenose shark (*Scoliodon laticaudus*) – LR/nt

Whitetip reef shark (*Triaenodon obesus*) – LR/nt

Family: Leptochariidae

Barbeled houndshark (*Leptocharias smithii*) – LR/nt

Family: Scyliorhinidae

Puffadder shyshark (*Haploblepharus edwardsii*) – LR/nt

Brown shyshark (*Haploblepharus fuscus)* – LR/nt

Pyjama shark (*Poroderma africanum)* – LR/nt

Narrowmouth catshark (*Schroederichthys bivius*) – LR/nt

Yellowspotted catshark (*Scyliorhinus capensis*) – LR/nt

Family: Sphyrnidae

Scalloped hammerhead shark (*Sphyrna lewini*) – LR/nt

Great hammerhead shark (*Sphyrna mokarran*) - DD

Bonnethead shark (*Sphyrna tiburo*) – LR/nt

Smooth hammerhead shark (*Sphyrna zygaena*) – LR/nt

Family: Triakidae

Whiskery shark (*Furgaleus macki*) – LR/cd

School shark/ Tope shark (*Galeorhinus galeus*) - VU A1bd

Whitefin topeshark (*Hemitriakis leucoperiptera*) - EN B1+2ce, C2b

Blacktip topeshark (*Hypogaleus hyugaensis*) – LR/nt

Gummy shark (*Mustelus antarcticus*) – LR/cd

Starry smoothound (*Mustelus asterias*) – LR/lc

Dusky smoothound (*Mustelus canis)* – LR/nt

Rig (*Mustelus lenticulatus*) – LR/cd

Common smoothhound (*Mustelus mustelus*) – LR/lc

Flapnose houndshark (*Scylliogaleus quecketti*) - VU B1+2c, C2b

Sharpfin houndshark (*Triakis acutipinna*) – VU C2b

Spotted gully shark (*Triakis megalopterus*) – LR/nt

Leopard shark (*Triakis semifasciata*) – LR/cd

Order: Heterodontiformes

Family: Heterodontidae

Horn shark (*Heterodontus francisci*) – LR/lc

Port Jackson shark (*Heterodontus portusjacksoni*) – LR/lc

Order: Hexanchiformes

Family: Hexanchidae

Bluntnose Sixgill shark (*Hexanchus griseus*) – LR/nt

Broadnose Sevengill shark (*Notorynchus cepedianus*) - DD

Order: Lamniformes

Family: Alopiidae

Thresher shark *(Alopias vulpinus)* - DD

Family: Cetorhinidae

Basking shark (*Cetorhinus maximus*) - VU A1ad + 2d

Family: Lamnidae

Great white shark (*Carcharodon carcharias*) – VU A1bcd + 2cd

Shortfin mako (*Isurus oxyrinchus)*- LR/nt

Salmon shark *(Lamna ditropis)* - DD

Porbeagle (*Lamna nasus*) – LR/nt

Family: Megachasmidae

Megamouth shark *(Megachasma pelagios)* - DD

Family: Odontaspididae

Bigeye sandtiger *(Odontaspis noronhai)* - DD

Family: Pseudocarchariidae

Crocodile shark (*Pseudocarcharias kamoharai)*- LR/nt

Family: Odontaspididae

Sand tiger shark/ Grey nurse shark (*Carcharias taurus*) – VU A1ab + 2d

Order: Orectolobiformes

Family: Brachaeluridae

Bluegray carpetshark *(Heteroscyllium colcloughi)* – VU C2b

Order: Orectolobiformes

Family: Rhincodontidae

Whale shark (*Rhincodon typus*) – VU A1bd + 2d

Order: Pristiophoriformes

Family: Pristiophoridae

Common sawshark (*Pristiophorus cirratus*) – LR/nt

Order: Squaliformes

Family: Dalatiidae

Kitefin shark (*Dalatias licha*) – DD

Order: Squaliformes

Family: Centrophoridae

Gulper shark *(Centrophorus granulosus)* – VU A1 abd + 2d

Order: Squaliformes

Family: Squalidae

Piked dogfish/ Spiny dogfish *(Squalus acanthias)* – LR/nt

Order: Squatiniformes

Family: Squatinidae

Argentine angel shark *(Squatina argentina)* – DD

Pacific angel shark *(Squatina californica)* – LR/nt

Angular angel shark *(Squatina guggenheim)* – VU A1bd + A2d

Smoothback angel shark *(Squatina occulta)* – EN A1 abd + A2d

Angel shark *(Squatina squatina)* – VU A1 abcd + A2d

Source: Anon (1996d). For further explanation of criteria and categories see Anon, 1994b:13-21.

9.0 LEGISLATION

Some countries have enacted legislation to conserve and manage shark stocks. In addition, legislation aimed at non-shark fisheries can have a positive effect upon shark conservation.

9.1 Europe

The Common Fisheries Policy (CFP) is a conservation policy aimed at regulating the quantities of fish caught, through a system of Total Allowable Catches (TACs) based on scientific advice. Each year TACs are allocated as quotas to Member States. They are complemented by a series of technical conservation measures intended to achieve more selective fishing, for example by setting rules on minimum landing sizes, minimum mesh sizes and gear design, as well as defining areas of seasonal closures, methods of fishing and target species. Opportunities to fish in third country waters are also secured through the CFP. A recent press release from the European Commission Directorate-General Fisheries (Anon 2000d) announced the publication of a Green Paper in early 2001 containing options for the future of the CFP which is up for review in 2002. Access to the North Sea by new Member States (Spain, Portugal, Sweden and Finland) after 2002 could deplete fish stocks further. Present restrictions on foreign fleet access to coastal waters could cease in 2001 although restrictions could be renewed for the next 10 years. Non-member state vessels are not permitted to fish within the member state's 12 mile coastal zone, where national legislation applies. However, national legislation does not apply in waters outside this zone. Non-member state vessels are only required to adhere to restrictions imposed by the CFP, although individual Member States can impose more restrictions, such as more detailed landing data, on its native fishers.

The European Union consists of Member States that must adhere to Regulations and must pass national laws to implement Directives. Non EU vessels fishing in EU waters will be required to sign up to some, if not all, of the Regulations.

The EU has passed legislation for the:

- provision of statistical landing data for listed species according to fishing zones[1]. Data is not recorded for fish discarded at sea, consumed on board or used as bait on board. These lists include species that are not on quota

---

[1] Council Regulations: 3880/91 (governs the Northeast Atlantic), 2018/93 (governs the Northwest Atlantic), 2597/95 (governs certain areas other than the North Atlantic)

- protection of juveniles of marine organisms, specifying mesh size and other fishing gear characteristics and fishing limitations, within certain areas and time-periods, with certain equipment[2].

- registration of fishing effort data in the logbook and the gathering of the effort data by the Member States for transmission to the Commission[3].

- prohibition from 1 January 2002 on landing bluntnose sixgill, basking, thresher, requiem, hammerhead, mackerel and mako sharks which have been caught in drift nets. This Regulation was aimed at reducing cetacean by-catch in tuna and swordfish fisheries. Sharks were listed to make it difficult for fishermen to evade the regulation. This does not constitute a global ban on drift nets as they may be used around estuaries in the NE coast of the UK and to capture migratory species such as salmon and bass in Skagerrak and Kattegat. Until 2002 Community vessels using drift nets must declare the quantities of each species caught and the catch dates and areas (except when in the Baltic sea). Drift net fishing in specified areas

---

[2] Council Regulation No 850/98
[3] Council Regulation No 2635/97

between 1 November and 31 January without an observer on board was also prohibited[4].

- all Community fishing vessels exceeding 24m length overall or 20m between perpendiculars and all vessels of third countries operating in Community waters must be equipped with a satellite tracking device enabling them to communicate to the Member States in whose waters they are carrying out their activities and to indicate their position at least once every two hours[5].

- enforcement of the UN Convention on International Trade in Endangered Species (CITES) (see section 10.1) and additional measures for the conservation of species in trade[6]. Annexes A to D contain the species listed in CITES Appendix I to IV. Additional species are also listed in Appendix A, B and D. As a result of the recent CITES listing (see section 10.1), the basking shark will be accepted onto Appendix C (possibly upgraded to Appendix B) by the end of 2000. No shark species are currently listed.

---

[4] Council Regulation No 1239/98
[5] Council Regulation No 2847/93
[6] Council Regulation No 338/97 as implemented by Council Regulation No 939/37

- listing of protected species and designation of conservation areas to provide a coherent European ecological network (Natura 2000)[7]. Some marine areas are listed but currently no shark species are.

- fixing quotas for certain fish stocks in Community waters[8]. When fishing within the 200 nautical mile zone off the coasts of the Member States of the Community the quantity of each species caught, the fishing method, the date and time and geographical position of the catch must be recorded. By-catch is regulated but not for sharks. Quotas are imposed for spurdog in the Skagerrak and Kattegat and North Sea in the following proportions:

Belgium	150
Denmark	863
Germany	156
France	276
The Netherlands	236
Sweden	12
United Kingdom	7177
EC	8870
Norway	600 (1)
Total Allowable Catch (TAC)	9470

---

[7] European Habitats and Species Directive
[8] Council Regulation No 2742/1999

All weights are in tonnes live weight. Norway's quota includes catches taken with long lines of grey shark and black shark, bird beak dogfish, leafscale gulper shark, greater lantern shark, smooth lantern shark and Portuguese dogfish. Norway has a quota of 100 tonnes weight of the basking shark liver but has not taken up its quota in recent years. Quantitative licences and fishing permits for third countries vessels in Community waters were issued such that Venezuela has 4 licences issued to fish for sharks in French Guyana waters. This quota does not constitute an acceptable management policy as it is not species specific.

- the UK to provide landing data on porbeagle, basking shark, spiny dogfish and Greenland shark as well as more general headings for dogfish sharks, dogfishes and hounds, various sharks and cartilaginous fishes[9].

The Bern Convention[10] has over 40 parties. In December 1997 the killing, capturing and keeping of the Mediterranean population of the basking shark was prohibited when they were added to Appendix II as a

---

[9] Council Regulation No 3880/91
[10] The Council of Europe Convention on the Conservation of European Wildlife and Natural Habitats

strictly protected species. Recently the Mediterranean population of the great white was also added to Appendix II. Appendix III requires the listed species to be subject to regulation if they are to be exploited and includes the Mediterranean populations of the shortfin mako, porbeagle, blue shark and angelshark. The EU has expressed a reservation on these new species such that no further species will be listed on the European Habitats and Species Directive until all the Member States have implemented the Directive into their national legislation and put Natura 2000 into place. Member States were given 2 years to implement the Directive in 1994 and some countries have yet to do so.

The Commission is considering setting up TACs for stocks of deep-water species in 2001 and has requested a discussion on the management of these resources at the next meeting of the North-East Atlantic Fisheries Commission in November 2000. The Commission is awaiting scientific advice on deep-water sharks. The Commission recognises that international cooperation is essential for the success of conservation measures for these species as the stocks concerned extend beyond Community waters (Anon 2000c).

The Commission is funding a project to improve the scientific basis for the management of elasmobranch fisheries (Development of Elasmobranch Assessments (DELASS)). The Commission are currently drafting plans to extend their statistics regulations to require landing data for elasmobranch species not currently listed and to publish identification guidelines (DG Statistics pers. comm.). To date, no elasmobranch management plans are in place (DG Fisheries, pers comm.).

The EU should adopt a management plan, employing the Precautionary Principle, for shark species in Community waters. Reducing shark by-catch should be a primary objective. The EU should seek the cooperation of the non-EU nations in the Mediterranean Sea and the Atlantic Ocean for species that range into the waters of third countries. European countries should ensure that their national fisheries legislation adequately addresses shark management.

9.11 United Kingdom

The three Marine Nature Reserves (MNRs) designated in UK waters since 1986 are unlikely to have had a measurable effect on elasmobranch stocks as no management measures were introduced with these stocks in mind. The same will probably be true for the greater number of Natura 2000 sites as they become operative (English Nature 1999a).

The Biodiversity Action Plan (HMSO 1994) is the Government's response to the UN Convention on Biological Diversity 1992 and lays emphasis on the UK's responsibility for conserving internationally threatened species. The basking shark, porbeagle, blue and soupfin sharks were listed on The UK Steering Group Report (Anon, 1995b) with the intention that action plans would be drawn up by the year 2000. To date, a basking shark plan was produced in 1999 along with two grouped species action plans for commercial marine fish and deep water fish, neither of which mention elasmobranchs but whose measures will have knock-on beneficial effects on the marine environment through minimum mesh size and other fishery controls. No statements or plans have been produced for the porbeagle, blue or soupfin but these may yet be produced depending on current research and surveys (English Nature pers. comm.).

In March 1998 the basking shark was awarded full protection in British waters (to 12 miles offshore) from intentional capture or disturbance in any place used as shelter or protection under a listing on Schedule 5, Wildlife and Countryside Act, 1981. The Countryside and Rights of Way Bill has been amended to include provisions for the protection of basking sharks from reckless disturbance wherever they may be. A government research project will shortly be put out to tender concerning basking shark range and population dynamics within the UK.

On 16 February 2000 the DETR announced the establishment of The National Wildlife Crime Unit which will comprise staff from several different agencies and deal mainly in crime relating to CITES trade issues (see 10.1) and rare native species.

In the UK the landing statistics required under EC legislation are collected through logbooks that the fishermen complete and send to the Ministry of Agriculture, Food and Fisheries (MAFF) through the Port Authority. In addition, the Sea Fisheries Inspectorate check landings at portside and carry out spot vessel checks, the Royal Navy also carry out spot vessel checks and sea helicopters check the presence of vessels. MAFF produced landing data for 1998 which listed angel shark, kitefin shark, leafscale gulper shark, great lantern shark, greater spotted dogfish, lesser spotted dogfish, spurdog (=spiny dogfish), birdbeak dogfish, Portuguese dogfish, longnose velvet dogfish, frilled shark, Greenland shark, sailfin roughshark, blackmouthed dogfish, blackbeak dogfish, tope, mako, sixgilled shark and knifetooth dogfish. Other shark and shark-like species are recorded under more general headings (MAFF Statistics pers. comm.). Porbeagle and basking shark were absent from this list but a spokesman from the MAFF statistics department recalled that these species had been listed in the past. He said that there was probably a recording error due to the fact that none of these species were landed during 1998 (MAFF Statistics pers comm.). Other species were listed with zero landings. An EC proposal, which would have extended landing data requirements for elasmobranch species and other fisheries species,[11] was supported by English Nature in 1995 (English Nature, pers.comm.) but rejected by MAFF due to economic feasibility. The UK should draft shark management plans and enforce them within coastal waters whilst petitioning the EC to extend these plans to cover the range of the managed shark population.

9.2 United States

9.21 Federal Plans

In 1993 the Atlantic Coast Shark Fisheries Management Plan began to quota regulate 39 species of sharks (22 large coastal, 7 small coastal and 10 pelagic) that occur in federal waters (beyond the three mile limit) to 200 miles inward, applying to the Gulf of Mexico, Caribbean and the Atlantic Ocean. A system of data collection and reporting was partially

---

[11] Proposal for a Council Regulation Establishing the List of Species to be Recorded in the Fisheries Logbook and Landing Declaration

implemented. Large coastal species are made up of the major sport and commercial target species such as the sandbar, blacktip, dusky, spinner, silky, bull, bignose, narrowtooth, Galapagos, night, reef, tiger, lemon, sand tiger, big tiger, nurse, scalloped hammerhead, smooth hammerhead, great hammerhead, great white, basking and whale. Small coastal species are caught primarily by recreational fishers and as by-catch to shrimp, longline and gillnet fisheries and include the Atlantic and Caribbean sharpnose, blacknose, finetooth, smalltail, bonnethead and angel. Pelagic species comprise offshore and deepwater species that are harvested primarily as by-catch of tuna and swordfish longline fisheries and are targeted by recreational fishermen, such as longfin and shortfin, porbeagle, common and bigeye threshers, oceanic whitetip, blue, bigeye, sixgill and sevengill sharks.

The plan initially envisaged a rapid population increase resulting in future increases to yield but contradictory evidence resulted in reductions to the maximum sustainable yield (MSY).

In April 1997, the National Marine Fisheries Service (NMFS) :

1. prohibited directed commercial and recreational fishing of five species of sharks: whale, basking, sand tiger, bigeye sand tiger,

and great white sharks (recreational catch-and-release for great white shark was permitted)

2. prohibited filleting of sharks at sea

3. required species-specific identification of all sharks landed

4. reduced the commercial quota for large coastal sharks by 50% to 1,285mt annually

5. established a commercial quota of 1,760mt for small coastal sharks

6. lowered the large coastal recreational TAC from 490t to 250t with a corresponding reduction in bag limit to two sharks of any category per vessel per trip plus two Atlantic sharpnose sharks per person per trip

Close attention must be paid to bag limits. As more recreational fishermen enter the fishery, the take will increase. Studies suggest that actual recreational landings for 1994 and 1995 greatly exceed the recreational allocation (Scott (1996), Scott, Phares & Slater (1996)), which would mean the current bag limits do not restrict the fishery to the TAC.

In 1999, NMFS added two additional species groups (prohibited species and deepwater/other sharks) and implemented limited access for the Atlantic commercial shark fishery. As of April 19, 2000, 281 fishermen had qualified to target sharks (directed permit) and 597 fishermen had qualified to land shark incidentally (incidental permit) (Anon, 2000). These numbers may increase as additional appeals are processed. Although the management unit is split into several species groups, any fisherman with a permit can land any species of shark (except prohibited species), within the appropriate retention limits. Fishermen without a permit are only authorized to land sharks under the recreational limit and cannot sell any sharks they land. The plan prohibits finning of all shark species in the Atlantic, Gulf of Mexico and Caribbean.

NMFS imposed a ban from 1 February 2001 on open water longline fishing off the entire Florida Atlantic coast along with DeSoto Canyon in the eastern Gulf of Mexico and a 3 month annual ban (February to April) in Charleston Bump off the coasts of Georgia and South Carolina.

The Western Pacific Pelagic Fisheries Management Plan includes thresher, requiem, mackerel and hammerhead sharks but these only represent a few shark species in the pelagic fisheries catch (Ito and

Machado, 1999). NMFS is preparing an environmental impact assessment on activities conducted under this plan. On 25 August 2000 an NMFS rule closed certain waters in the central and north Pacific Ocean to longline fishing, imposed fishing gear restrictions, effort limits, fish sale restrictions, catch reporting requirements and increased observer coverage in the Hawaii-based pelagic longline fishery. Federal regulation of shark fisheries in the Pacific has a long way to go to catch up with federal regulation in the Atlantic.

On 6 June 2000 the Shark Finning Prohibition Act (HR 3535) which calls on federal and state agencies to ban shark finning in all US waters was passed by the US House of Representatives and moved to the US Senate for consideration.

The Magnuson-Stevens Fishery Conservation and Management Act, the law governing the federal management of marine fisheries, is currently up for re-authorisation. One of the bills before Congress is the Fisheries Recovery Act (HR 4046) which will strengthen the conservation provisions added by the Sustainable Fisheries Act in 1996. This bill supports the re-authorisation agenda adopted by the Marine Fish Conservation Network.

NMFS has been conducting research with Canada and with Mexico to establish management plans for shared stocks and an age and growth study of porbeagle sharks with Canada.

9.22 State Plans

In 1998 the Ocean Wildlife Campaign criticised Atlantic Coast and Gulf Coast states for undermining the NMFS plan by not enacting complimentary state regulations (14% of commercial and 64% of recreational catches occur in state-controlled waters). The report states that sharks are being overfished and caught in by-catch in state waters where the federal rules do not apply, and that bays and estuaries are being destroyed so reducing nursery grounds. New Jersey and Louisiana have two of the largest shark fisheries but no shark management whatsoever (Anon, 1998b). Strict quotas for spiny dogfish in the US Atlantic have recently been enacted but the State of Massachusetts has since announced a state water limit nearly twice the quota for the entire Atlantic coast.

Several states (Virginia, North Carolina, California, Texas and Florida) have enacted laws to regulate shark fishing in their respective regions. On 1st January 1994 the State of California made it illegal to take or to trade in white sharks from its waters except with a special permit or as incidental catch in selected net fisheries (State Assembly Bill AB 522). Grey nurse sharks and great white sharks are fully protected in Florida and California. In Florida State waters, the basking shark is fully protected out to the three mile limit on the east coast and nine miles on the Gulf coast. In 1998 Alaska closed state waters to commercial shark fishing and set strict recreational bag limits.

On 22 June 2000 a state bill was passed to prohibit the landing of any shark fins in the state of Hawaii unless the shark is landed whole. On 23 June 2000 a rule was passed banning longlining vessels from a 2.5 million square mile area north of Hawaii and limiting each vessel to approximately six days of fishing in 4 million square miles of ocean south of Hawaii with no fishing during April or May and a federal observer to be on board each vessel.

The US Atlantic Coast Shark Fisheries Management Plan is the leading shark fisheries management regime in the world. However, management plans are needed for state-controlled waters and for the Pacific.

9.3 South Africa

On 11th April 1991, legislation was passed to protect the white shark in South African waters prohibiting catches within 200 miles of the South African coast and subsequent sale. Permits are issued only for research purposes or to the Natal Sharks Board (Cherry, 1991). In 1998 the Marine Living Resources Act made it illegal to handle or attract white sharks without a permit and imposed adherence to a Code of Conduct. Grey nurse sharks are also fully protected.

9.4 Maldives

On 5 June 1995 15 top diving sites were declared Marine Protected Areas and whale shark fishing was banned. Plans are being considered to protect more dive sites as well as much larger reef areas (Anderson and Maniku, 1996:14) which will act to conserve sharks and increase revenue through diving. Grey nurse sharks are fully protected.

9.5 Canada

The Department of Fisheries and Oceans (DFO) banned the finning of sharks on June 6, 1994. The DFO have also produced a shark conservation and management plan for controlling and monitoring fisheries for shortfin mako, porbeagle, and blue shark. The DFO have established a regional assessment process and have been working on a 2000-2001 Shark Management Plan.

9.6 Australia

In April 1988 the Federal Government introduced a management plan into the southern shark fishery based on restrictions on boat numbers and gill-netting (McGregor, 1988:2-7). In 1991 criteria were introduced to control State and Federal longline fisheries (Campbell et.al. 1992:251-62). In 1996, the effort in the southern shark fishery was less than half the peak effort of 1987, partly due to a reduction in the amount of net permitted per fishing operation (Walker et al. 1998). In Western Australia, there has also been a significant reduction in effort through gear reduction. The management intent is a 50% reduction of effort on 1993/94 levels by 2000/01 (WA State of Fisheries Report 1997/98). All Australian fisheries should employ similar methods.

Finning has been banned in NSW. It is prohibited in NSW waters to take and land any shark species mutilated in any manner other than by heading, gutting or removing gills or for any boat in NSW waters to possess shark fins on board.

Since the early 1960s certain bays and estuaries around Tasmania have been designated shark nursery areas, where the taking of either the school shark or the gummy shark is prohibited. However, in the past, poaching could not be controlled because the use of shark-fishing gear had not been prohibited, and gill-netting by both recreational and commercial fishers was permitted (Anon, 1989). This situation has been rectified by the National Representative System of Marine Protected Areas (NRSMPA) (see Appendix 7) set up in 1991.

There has been ban on shark gill-netting and long-lining within 3 nautical miles (nm) of the Victorian coast since 1988. Small white sharks appear to occur reasonably frequently in some coastal areas of Victoria and this ban may provide a refuge for white sharks at a size when they are most susceptible to capture in nets and longlines.

In December 1997 the grey nurse and white shark were listed as 'vulnerable' under Schedule 1 Part 2 of the Endangered Species Act 1992 which excludes taking or killing in Australian Commonwealth waters (from 3 nautical miles offshore to the edge of the continental shelf or the Australian Fishing Zone, whichever is greater) without a scientific permit. The Act identifies the need for recovery plans and specifies the content of the plan. Draft recovery plans were written for both these species in 2000 (see Appendices 2 and 3). The Environmental Protection and Biodiversity Conservation Act 1999 (EPBC 1999) came into force on 17 July 2000 and repealed the

Endangered Species Act. Both the white shark and the nurse shark are listed as 'vulnerable' under Part 13. The EPBC 1999 states that however a listed species is taken, it must be reported to the Secretary of Environment Australia within 7 days. The requirement to report incidental catch is not apparent in any of the state legislation.

Every state within the normal Australian range of the white shark has specific white shark protection measures. The white shark is fully protected in Tasmania, South Australia and Victoria; commercially protected in Western Australia; protected in NSW and Queensland but with exemptions for beach meshing operations (Bruce and Stevens 1998) (see Appendix 1). Additional listings under state threatened species legislation is being considered by Tasmania and Victoria. White sharks are listed in the 'Uncertain Status' category by the Australian Society of Fish Biology (they are considering a revision of the white shark's status to 'vulnerable'). Trade in South Australia of white shark products by commercial fisheries is outlawed (Presser and Allen, 1995).

Grey nurse sharks are protected in NSW (Fisheries Management Act 1994), Tasmania (Fisheries Regulations 1996) and Queensland (Fisheries Act 1994 (Fisheries Regulation 1995)) and listed in the vulnerable status category by the Australian Society of Fish Biology.

A seasonal aggregation of whale sharks in the Ningaloo Marine Park from March to May each year prompted a management plan initiative in 1998 to establish necessary research and management control and monitoring. The whale shark is protected in Western Australia.

Finning should be banned in Australian Commonwealth waters and in all State waters. State waters should also extend their species specific protection measures. The EPBC 1999 'vulnerable' list should be extended to cover more shark species which would prompt more recovery plans.

9.7 New Zealand

The Fisheries Act 1983 affords partial protection to several fish species including the basking shark. Commercial target fishing for the species has been banned since 1991 although they may be taken as by-catch following which the liver and fins are sold, often exported.

The possession of a quota to fish a certain species does not allow fishermen to fish without regard to other species they might take as by-catch. The quota management system contains a legal obligation for fishermen to have access to quota to cover the by-catch of any Individual Transferable Quota (ITQ) species. In the event that a fisherman over catches their by-catch quota they may trade this for an amount of uncaught target quota under the by-catch trade off agreement. School shark and rig are ITQ species. Some species such as spiny dogfish have quotas imposed each year but do not form part of the ITQ system (Sant & Hayes, 1996). Other fisheries could employ ITQs to control and monitor their by-catch.

9.8 Ecuador

The Special Law for Galapagos, passed by the Ecuadorean Congress in 1997, established the Galapagos Marine Reserve in 1998. The law banned industrial fishing in the reserve, which involved mostly purse-seining for tuna and longlining for tuna, billfish and sharks. Artisanal fishing by locals is still allowed. Current enforcement is insufficient as the law is flouted by commercial fisheries. On 24 November 1999 an Ecuadorean fishing vessel was found in the National Park using a 20 mile longline which caught scalloped hammerheads, blacktip, whitetip reef and blue sharks.

9.9 Philippines

The Fishery Administration Order No 193 (26 March 1998) prohibits the catch, sale, purchase and possession, transport and export of whale sharks. This ban affects all of the Philippines including the Donsol and the traditional Bohol Sea whaling and shark fishing communities. This law is regularly flouted (see 5.28).

10.0 INTERNATIONAL SPECIES PROTECTION

Although international conventions are voluntary codes of practice and have no force of law, many have indirectly aided shark conservation by addressing fisheries and environmental concerns.

In December 1991 the UN[12] opted to reduce large-scale pelagic driftnet fishing by 50% by 30 June 1992 and to introduce a complete phase out by the end of 1992. The General Assembly reaffirmed the importance of this resolution in their December 1996 meeting stating that a biennial report be submitted on it's progress (UN Press Release 1996). This is a very important step as the International North Pacific Fisheries Commission estimated that the high seas driftnet fishery for squid caught 1.8 million blue sharks and nearly 140,000 salmon sharks in 1990 alone (Bonfil, 1994).

The Rio Convention[13] aims for "the conservation of biological diversity, the sustainable use of its components and the fair and equitable sharing of the benefits arising out of the utilization of genetic resources". The Convention was followed up through the United Nations General Assembly Special Sessions (UNGASS) which in June 1997 declared "an

---

[12] General Assembly of the United Nations adopted Resolution 46/215
[13] The UN Convention on Biological Diversity - entered into force December 1993

urgent need for ... Governments to prevent or eliminate overfishing and excessive fishing capacity...".

In 1994 the UN[14] required all members of the international community to cooperate in the conservation and management of the living resources of the seas and oceans. This was elaborated in 1995 with the UN Migratory Fish Stocks Convention[15]. The Multilateral High-Level Conference on the Conservation and Management of Highly Migratory Fish Stocks in the Western and Central Pacific had its sixth meeting in Hawaii in April 2000 and negotiations continue between the 27 countries to develop a new convention.

The "Bergen conclusions"[16] are political statements that focus specifically on the integration of fisheries and environmental issues. A Guidance Note published in March 1998 summarises the actions and initiatives taken to implement the Bergen conclusions which includes conservation measures to reduce catch of immature fish and discarding.

UNEP's Regional Seas Programme protects shared marine and water resources through Conventions. These provide the legal framework for regional Action Plans covering 140 countries. In 1999 the Barcelona

---

[14] The UN Convention on the Law of the Sea – entered into force November 1994 and currently has 166 parties
[15] The UN Convention of Straddling Fish Stocks and Highly Migratory Fish Stocks – adopted in 1995

Convention[17] added the basking and great white sharks to Annex II (full protection in the Mediterranean Sea) and the shortfin mako, porbeagle, blue and angel sharks to Annex III (partial protection in the Mediterranean Sea in the form of fisheries regulation).

The Bonn Convention[18] "recognizes that the States are and must be the protectors of the migratory species of wild animals that live within or pass through their national jurisdictional boundaries". In November 1999 the whale shark was added to Appendix II so recognising that the species has an unfavourable conservation status that would benefit from co-operative action between party states.

Other international bodies undertaking shark conservation projects include:

- the International Convention for the Conservation of Atlantic Tunas (ICCAT) which initiated a data collection effort for member countries to provide species-specific information on sharks caught as a by-catch in tuna fisheries in the Atlantic Ocean.

---

[16] Adopted at The Intermediate Ministerial Meeting of the North Sea Conferences in March 1997

[17] The UNEP Barcelona Convention for the Protection of the Mediterranean Sea

- the Latin American Organisation for Fishery Development (OLDEPESCA) which solicited information about sharks in the region of the Latin American Economic System.

- the Indian Ocean Tuna Commission (1996) which recommended that all countries fishing for tuna and tuna-like species in the Indian Ocean provide data on by-catch and discards of sharks and non-tuna species.

- ICES and ICCAT which recently discussed cooperation in the assessment of pelagic sharks.

- Northwest Atlantic Fisheries Organisation (NAFO) Scientific Council which agreed in June 2000 to provide management advice on elasmobranchs.

(see Annex 3 for further details)

10.1 United Nations Convention on International Trade in Endangered Species of Wild Fauna and Flora (CITES)

CITES will be considered in more detail as it has been the focus of much shark debate in recent years. CITES came into force in 1975 and

---

[18] The UN Convention on the Conservation of Migratory Species of Wild Animals – entered into force November 1983 and currently has 56 parties

regulates international trade in animal and plant species through import and export permits. At present 151 countries are party to CITES. The species protected are listed under 3 appendices (Table 10.11), which are based on scientific criteria submitted by the Animals and Plants Committees. Proposals to amend the appendices, and new resolutions on the implementation of the Convention, are considered at biennial conferences.

Table 10.11 CITES Appendices

Appendix I - lists species threatened with extinction and subject to international trade. Trade in artificially propagated or captive bred specimens is allowed subject to license. Requires both an export and an import permit.
Appendix II - lists species that may become threatened with extinction if trade is not regulated. Trade in wild, captive bred, and artificially propagated specimens is allowed subject to license. Requires an export permit.
Appendix III - lists species not threatened worldwide but protected within individual party states. These states need the help of other parties to control trade in the affected species. Requires export permits.
Source: Anon, 1996f

The 9th Conference of the Parties 1994 passed Resolution Conf. 9.17 on the "Status of International Trade in Shark Species" (see Appendix 4) to improve international shark-data collection and review the biological status of sharks and the effects of global trade. At the Animals Committee meeting in September 1996 it was decided that the parties would gather information on international shark trade for analysis and reporting by the Governments of the U.S. and Panama. At the 10th Conference of the Parties 1997 a document was submitted by the Animals Committee on the biological and trade status of sharks and recommendations were endorsed to implement Resolution Conf. 9.17 (res. 10.73 and 10.74). In 1998 the FAO commissioned several studies in different regions on shark stocks and fisheries in order to develop management plans and the CITES Animals Committee pursued parallel investigations into threats to sharks.

In 1999 the FAO produced the United Nations International Plan of Action for the Conservation and Management of Sharks (IPOA-Sharks). Its objective is to ensure the conservation and management of sharks and their long-term sustainable use. (For aims of a National Shark-Plan see Appendix 5). It is a voluntary plan which applies to States in the waters of which sharks are caught commercially or incidentally by their own or foreign vessels and to States the vessels of which catch sharks commercially or incidentally on the high seas. The FAO is developing Technical Guidelines to assist States in the development and implementation of their shark plans. Each applicable State is responsible for developing, implementing and monitoring a shark plan which should be in force by the FAO Committee on Fisheries (COFI) session in 2001. COFI will report biennially on the state of progress on the implementation of the IPOA-Sharks.

The USA has prepared a draft plan of action and Australia has prepared draft recovery plans for the nurse shark and great white shark. The European Commission intends to draw up a plan for sharks on behalf of all of the Member States and is currently gathering information for submission to the UN in 2001. A workshop on the sustainable management of sharks in West Africa was held in April 2000 so that recommendations can result in a plan of action. In their 2000 report the ICES Study Group on Elasmobranch Fishes expressed concern at the lack of progress in implementing the IPOA-Sharks by both member countries and the FAO.

The 11th Conference of the Parties[19] received three proposals for shark listings that were supported by TRAFFIC and the IUCN Shark

---

[19] held at Gigiri, Kenya, 10-20 April 2000

Specialist Group. All three were rejected despite the great white shark proposal being resubmitted as an Appendix II listing.

Table 10.12 CITES 2000 Shark Proposals at the 11th Conference of the Parties

Species	Country	Proposal	Result
Prop. 11.47 *Rhincodon typus* Whale shark	USA	Included in App. II	REJECTED
Prop. 11.48 *Carcharodon carcharias* Great white shark	AUSTRALIA, USA	Included in App. I Resubmitted as inclusion in App. II	REJECTED on both proposals
Prop. 11.49 *Cetorhinus maximus* Basking shark	UNITED KINGDOM	Included in App. II	REJECTED

Species can be added to Appendix III on the request of an individual party: no discussion of the proposal is required. Following a request from the UK the basking shark was accepted onto Appendix III on 13th September 2000. This requires that all parties report their trade in, and issue export permits for, basking shark. The trade data generated will aid discussion at the 12th Conference of the Parties in 2002 on whether the basking shark should be listed on Appendix II or I.

The wide-ranging habits of many sharks and the lack of shark legislation and enforcement in many countries require legislation on a global scale. Prohibition of trade in sharks and shark products would also help to prevent illegal fishing in the guise of incidental by-catch. Governments are required to submit reports, including trade records, to the CITES Secretariat in Switzerland. If tables were compiled for the global shark trade it would be possible for conservation bodies to identify over-exploited shark populations through changes in the trade of species-specific products. A listing on CITES would not eradicate the trade in shark parts, but would make the trade less commercially viable and drive it underground. Enforcement of CITES is the responsibility of member states hence low regulation occurs in poor or corrupt States.

11.0 DETAILED CASE STUDIES OF THE BASKING SHARK (*Cetorhinus maximus*) AND THE GREAT WHITE SHARK (*Carcharodon carcharias*)

The basking shark and the great white shark both belong to the order Lamniformes, are both listed as 'vulnerable' on the 2000 IUCN Red List, have similar distributions (Table 11.1), migratory distances and reproductive strategies, yet have very different behaviour (the basking shark is a filter-feeder and the white shark an apex predator). The basking shark is targeted by man for its fisheries and the white shark is targeted due to its man-eating reputation.

Table 11.1 Centres of abundance for great white sharks and basking sharks

Geographic Region	Great White Shark	Basking Shark
Western Atlantic	Newfoundland to Florida, Bahamas, Cuba, northern Gulf of Mexico; Brazil and Argentina,	Newfoundland to Florida and southern Brazil to Argentina
Eastern Atlantic	France to Mediterranean, Madeira, Canary Islands, Senegal, Ghana, Zaire; Western Cape Province, South Africa.	Iceland, Norway and western Barents Sea to Mediterranean and Senegal, and the Western Cape Province, South Africa

Western Indian Ocean	South Africa, Seychelles Islands, Red Sea.	Eastern Cape Province, South Africa
Western Pacific	Siberia (USSR), Japan, the Koreas, China, Bonin Island, the Philippines; Indonesia, Australia (Queensland, New South Wales, Victoria, Tasmania, South and Western Australia), New Zealand, New Caledonia	Japan, the Koreas, China, Australia (New South Wales, Victoria, Tasmania, South and Western Australia), New Zealand
Central Pacific	Marshall Islands, Hawaiian Islands	One washed up in Hawaii[20]
Eastern Pacific	Gulf of Alaska to Gulf of California; Panama to Chile.	Gulf of Alaska to the Gulf of California

Source: Compagno, 1984:239 & 234

11.1 Basking Shark (*Cetorhinus maximus*)

Order Lamniformes

Family Cetorhinidae

At 10-11m maximum length the basking shark is the second largest fish after the whale shark. It is one of three species of huge, filter-feeding sharks, the other two being the megamouth and the whale shark. The basking shark is unique in relying entirely on the passive flow of water

---

[20] Sarah Fowler, pers comm

through its pharynx, generated by swimming, for filtration of plankton and crustaceans by its gillrakers.

11.11 Distribution

Basking sharks have an extensive range within coastal and continental shelf regions of temperate waters in the Atlantic and Pacific Oceans and the Mediterranean, although its distribution in deeper waters is unknown. In Great Britain the basking shark is observed from May to September off the south and west coasts from Dorset to northern Scotland, particularly the south coasts of Devon and Cornwall, off the west coast of the Isle of Man and around the Isle of Arran in the Clyde estuary. In addition to the centres of abundance listed in Table 11.1 the basking shark is found in Ecuador, Peru and Chile and possibly the Galapagos Islands (Compagno, 1984:234). The winter distribution of basking sharks is unknown other than appearances around Monterey Bay, California (Squire, 1967:247-250).

11.12 Migrations

Basking sharks are highly migratory with seasonal population movements inshore to feed on high abundances of zooplankton near tidal fronts in coastal areas. Off the Atlantic seaboard of North America they appear in the southern part of their range in spring (North Carolina to New York), apparently shift northward in summer (New England and

Canada), and disappear in autumn and winter. Off the eastern North Pacific basking sharks occur in greatest numbers during autumn and winter in the southernmost part of their range (California), but shift to more northern latitudes in spring and summer (up to Washington and British Columbia). Off the British Isles the bulk of the population appears in the springtime, apparently engaging in courtship activity and copulation, and disappears by the autumn.

Migrations may be age- and sex-segregated. Watkins (1958) recorded commercial catches from surface basking sharks in Scotland in summer to be about 95% females and observations made in the Isle of Man waters indicate that the sex ratio is similarly skewed. If this sex ratio is exhibited throughout the UK, removal of large numbers of mature females could have serious consequences to the population as a whole. Pregnant females are almost entirely unknown for the species, suggesting that such females are spatially and bathymetrically separated from those members of the population that are regularly seen basking at the surface. Juveniles below 3m long are also extremely rare. Inadvertent sub-surface catches from around Newfoundland give a sex ratio of just over two males per female (Lien and Fawcett, 1986:246-252) and it is possible that, in the normal course of events, male basking sharks swim deeper than females and are not as evident at the surface.

Bigelow *et al* (1948) stated that a lack of evidence in the Atlantic for any southward increase in abundance during autumn and winter suggests that they simply disperse offshore and overwinter in deeper waters, lying inactive or close to the bottom. As squalene is found in large quantities only in the livers of deep-water sharks (Baldridge, 1972:306-324), the presence of an intermediate level, as found in basking sharks, provides circumstantial evidence for the adoption of at least a moderately deep water habit for a part of their life-history.

It is generally assumed that the return of the sharks to coastal waters during spring is associated with periods of high biological production when supplies of their planktonic prey are plentiful (Kunzlik, 1988:9). It also appears that temperature may affect their distribution. In discussing incidental captures off the coast of Newfoundland, Lien and Fawcett (1986:246-252) found that captures rarely occurred until water temperatures reached 6°C and were not common until a temperature of 8°C was reached; 90% of captures were made at temperatures between 8°C and 12°C. Although these water temperatures may merely correlate with the normal seasonal appearance of basking sharks and not be the cause of it, it is interesting to note that at Monterey Bay, California, where they are most abundant during winter, they are least abundant when water temperatures are close to or greater than 14°C (Squire,

1967:247-250). It is possible that such temperature effects explain the absence of basking sharks from tropical waters.

This species may spend as much as 50% of its time in deep water beyond the scope of most fisheries. Part of this time may be spent giving birth. Future risk will arise from increased coastal and deep-water fisheries (English Nature 1999a).

11.13 Diet
Recognisable food items in the stomach include copepods, arrow-worms, larval crustacea and fish eggs (Matthews and Parker, 1950:535-576; Parker and Boesman, 1954:185-194). It is not known why basking sharks favour the surface when greater plankton concentrations may be found deeper in the water column (Maxwell, 1952). Plankton densities seasonally fall below levels thought essential to maintain ordinary swimming and metabolic activity in this shark. Hybernation or benthic feeding have been suggested as alternative strategies until plankton blooms reoccur and rakers are replaced. Alternatively, the massive oil-filled liver of this species may supply energy to support a reduced rate of activity (slower swimming in colder, deep water) while gillrakers and plankton supplies regenerate. Some specimens caught in the north-east Atlantic in winter had shed their gillrakers, possibly indicating inactivity in deep water when low zooplankton populations in winter

make feeding activity inefficient (Fowler, 1996). Studies in the English Channel show that they exhibit selective foraging behaviour on productive zooplankton patches along thermal fronts, track tidally controlled movements of patches, and follow frontal boundaries as they move. These findings and the apparent unpredictability in surface sightings suggest basking sharks are dependent on enhanced productivity found near transient oceanographic features. Consequently, population trends in the north-east Atlantic will be linked with broad-scale changes in secondary production and controlling factors e.g. summer stratification and North Atlantic Oscillation (NAO) (English Nature, 1999a).

11.14 Growth and Reproduction

Males mature at about 4 or 5m and reach about 9m, females mature at 8.1 to 9.8m (Compagno, 1984:236). It is presumed that the basking shark is ovoviviparous like other lamnoids. The assumption of ovoviviparity is supported by a report of a Norwegian fisherman catching a female specimen which proceeded to give birth to five live young and one still-born, estimated to be between 1.5 and 2m long (Sund, 1943:285-286). The gestation period is unknown, although Parker and Stott (1965:305-319) suggest a period of 3.5 years based upon their postulated age-length relationship for this species. Nursery zones have not been identified due to few sightings of juveniles.

Age has been estimated by counting vertebral rings and attempting to correlate them with supposed changes in size of individuals within a population. It has been suggested that two calcified rings are laid down per year until maturity at between 6 or 7 years for males (Parker and Stott 1965). The biannual calibration of the rings is uncertain and controversial. A yearly rate of ring deposition has been suggested, with possible age at maturity for males doubled to 12 to 16 or more years.

11.15 Population Structure

Census data of the abundance of basking sharks in localised areas are limited in value as the number observed or estimated to be present at the time of the survey may reflect the erratic nature of the inshore invasions rather than changes in stock size or trends in abundance. Some argue that basking sharks probably do not form locally discrete stocks (Kunzlik, 1990). However, there is contrary evidence that fisheries targeting of basking shark can result in a severe depletion of stock and a failure to recover. In the 1950s a basking shark eradication programme was carried out in Barkley Sound, Vancouver Island, in response to Canadian fishermen who complained that basking sharks kept getting caught in their nets. Several hundred sharks were killed (Clemens and Wilby, 1961) and it appears the population has not yet recovered.

11.16 Fisheries

It has been argued that the erratic nature of basking shark seasonal appearances, coupled with marketing and economic difficulties, caused the failure of earlier UK fisheries and contributed to the decline of the post-war Irish fishery. The seasonal inshore movements of basking sharks can be highly erratic, and harpoon fisheries for the species are restricted by a requirement for calm, sunny conditions. European fisheries were severely restricted in the late 1980s owing to a collapse in the market for liver oil (Kunzlik, 1990:17). The basking shark is extremely vulnerable to overfishing due to its slow growth rate, lengthy maturation time, long gestation period and probable low fecundity. It is difficult to ascertain whether overfishing contributed to the fisheries collapse, though given the high numbers landed and the low viability of the species it is likely to be a factor.

A trade in basking shark fins existed earlier this century between Ireland and Hong Kong (McNally, 1976) and potential exists for an upsurge in trade of fins from basking sharks taken in UK waters. Basking shark meat is used for human consumption either fresh or dried salted, fins are used for shark fin soup, the hide is used for leather, the carcass for fishmeal and oil, which is extracted from the liver for its high squalene content (about 50 per cent, Stevens, 1987:192), was formerly used for tanning leather and lamp oil. The price for dry basking shark fins is approximately £80 per Kg (Rose, 1996). Each whole shark is worth at least £1,000 (Hancox, 1994).

The species has been exploited by man for several centuries. During the last century basking sharks were harpooned by whaling vessels. Today, basking sharks are the object of smallscale harpoon fisheries from small boats off Iceland, California, Peru and Ecuador and are currently heavily fished off China and Japan. Nets, such as bottom gillnets and bottom and pelagic trawls, are also used to fish basking sharks. Entanglement in net gear has resulted in significant incidental catches, such as 77-120 sharks taken annually in a bottom set gill net fishery in the Celtic Sea (Fowler, 1996).

11.161 California

Between 1924 and 1937 a small enterprise was established off the Californian coast catching basking sharks for reduction to fishmeal and for the sale of shark liver oil as a "cure-all" tonic (McCormick, Allen and Young, 1964). Off Monterey Bay, California, up to 200 basking sharks were taken annually using aircraft spotters and harpoons from 1946 to 1949 (Roedel and Ripley, 1950).

11.162 Norway

Norwegian fishermen are known to have been actively fishing for porbeagle sharks off the Scottish coast as early as 1934, although it is not known when they first started fishing there for basking sharks. In UK waters Norwegian vessels may not fish within the 12 mile coastal zone. Norway is the only Member State with an EC quota for basking shark. The quota allows a TAC of 100 mt of liver annually which was used mainly for shark liver oil and the shark fin soup market. Catches declined steadily with an annual catch of about 500 sharks in 1987 although this may be attributed to market forces and the rationalization of the Norwegian fleet (Kunzlik, 1988). In 1995 the fishery reported a very poor season with few sharks being seen (Sharkwatch, 1995). The market for shark liver oil began to drop in 1995 such that the hunting continued mainly to supply the shark fin soup market. In the past few years Norway has not taken up its EC quota.

11.163 Scotland

A one man basking shark harpoon fishery was run off the west coast of Scotland by Howard McCrindle. Between 1983 and 1994 he landed about 440 basking sharks, mainly sexually mature females, between 20 and 35 feet long and weighing four to seven tonnes. Taken along with losses in drift nets and those shot by Norwegians an estimated 400 basking sharks per annum were taken from waters around Britain before

UK coastal water protection was passed and Norway stopped utilising its EC quota (Marine Conservation Society pers.comm.).

11.164 Ireland

In 1947 a fishery using specially constructed nets to capture basking sharks was established on the west coast of Ireland at Keem Bay, Achill Island. Nets and harpoons were used in the developmental years of the fishery, but by 1951 nets alone were used either to actively encircle a previously spotted shark or to entangle sharks in set nets as they swam around the margins of the bay (McNally, 1976). Harpoons were reintroduced to the Irish west coast fishery in 1973. The following two years saw 17 and 36 sharks respectively caught in addition to those netted (see Table 11.1641). These years also saw the establishment of an Irish harpoon fishery off the south-east coast of Ireland which contributed to a catch of 180 and 350 sharks (McNally, 1976).

The level of Norwegian catch increased substantially around the time the Achill catch declined (Table 11.1641) suggesting that the sharks were intercepted before reaching the confines of Keem Bay. However, the harpoon fishery off the south-east coast of Ireland managed substantial catches in 1974 and 1975. The decline in Achill shark catches was paralleled by a decline in zooplankton in the north-east Atlantic over the same 38 year period, emphasising the importance of food availability in controlling basking shark movement. To elucidate the relative importance of pressures on basking shark fisheries it is necessary to compare the fishery efforts (CPUE) of all 3 fisheries against one another and against measures of food availability, whilst taking into account the geographical and temporal range of each fishery. It will then be possible to estimate the contribution from overfishing to the decline of these fisheries and to provide an indication of whether basking sharks form locally discrete stocks.

Table 11.1641 Commercial basking shark catches (numbers) 1947-1975

Year	Ireland (Achill)	Norway
1947	6	250
1948	80	964
1949	450	782
1950	905	1,764
1951	1,630	806
1952	1,808	392
1953	1,068	596
1954	1,162	682
1955	1,708	294
1956	977	528
1957	468	258
1958	500	122
1959	280	2,532
1960	219	4,266
1961	258	2,042
1962	116	1,266
1963	75	2,210
1964	39	2,138
1965	47	1,304
1966	46	1,822
1967	41	4,180
1968	75	3,160
1969	113	3,130
1970	42	3,774
1971	29	1,708
1972	62	1,438
1973	85	2,214
1974	33	2,148
1975	38	3,670

Sources: McNally (1976); Norges Fiskeristatistikk; Norges Fiskeridirektoratet; Norges Fiskerier.

11.17 Protection

The basking shark has received full protection in the UK, US Atlantic, Florida, Isle of Man and Guernsey, and partial protection in New Zealand. It is listed on the EC driftnet ban and the EC Bern Convention with a future listing on the EC Habitats and Species Directive and will shortly be listed on CITES Appendix III. The EC requires annual landing data from the Member States for basking shark landings and the UK wrote a basking shark plan in 1999 (for further details see section 9 'Legislation'). The basking shark is also listed on the UN Barcelona Convention (for further details see section 10 'International Species Protection').

11.18 Future Recommendations

The basking shark CITES listing should be changed to a listing on Appendix I until more is known about this species and how to manage it. The Countryside and Rights of Way Bill should be adopted to outlaw disturbances to basking sharks and a Code of Conduct should be drawn up to reduce harassment. A decline in numbers has been recorded around the Isle of Man despite full protection in its waters, presumably because individuals are caught when they move outside the small area of sea where protection is in operation. UK legislation is prone to similar undermining by fishing outside of the protected UK coastal zone.

Protection in Eire coastal waters, the extension of UK protection to Northern Ireland and the withdrawal of Norway's EC basking shark quota would protect the whole of the Irish Sea and prevent undermining of both the Isle of Man and UK protection zones.

Research should be conducted into the basking shark's life cycle, migration patterns, over-wintering areas, population dynamics and mating and nursery zones. Vulnerable areas must be protected. Fishery log books and public sighting sheets would assist in gathering information as would autopsies on sharks from incidental or commercial fisheries. Genetic studies would help to ascertain population structure.

11.2 Great White Shark (*Carcharodon carcharias*)

Order Lamniformes

Family Lamnidae

The great white shark, commonly called the white shark, is the largest predatory fish in the ocean. It has a heat-exchanging circulatory system allowing it to maintain body temperatures up to 14 degrees centigrade above that of the surrounding seawater so permitting a higher level of activity (Goldman *et al* 1996).

11.21 Diet
Prey includes a wide range of bony and Chondrichthyian fishes, chelonians, cephalopods, molluscs, crustaceans, avians, sea turtles and marine mammals (Compagno, 1984:239). Sea otters are commonly killed by great white sharks off California, but have yet to be found as stomach contents (Ames *et.al*., 1980:196-209). Great white sharks appear to exhibit an age/size preference for certain foods with a preference for fish in the juvenile stage (less than 2.2 metres) (Klimley 1994, Bruce 1992) and other sharks, rays and marine mammals in more mature sharks. Great white sharks may prefer energy-rich marine mammals to other comparatively energy-deficient species as they have been observed feeding on baleen whale blubber in preference to the muscle (Klimley,1994:129).

11.22 Distribution
The white shark is found in temperate and subtropical waters throughout the world and is most frequently encountered off South Africa, southern Australia, northern California, and the northeastern United States (Last & Stevens 1994). Whilst principally an epipelagic dweller of neritic waters, the great white is found from the surface to 1280m depth (Stevens, 1987:28), and from the surfline to well offshore, as well as frequenting enclosed bays and offshore continental islands, particularly those with pinniped colonies. The extensive coastal range of

the white shark and the occurrence of large individuals off mid-ocean archipelagos suggest that it undertakes trans-oceanic movements (Fergusson et al., 1996:1).

11.23 Migrations
Pronounced periodicity in great white abundance in some areas may be correlated with temperature and life stage. Off Natal, South Africa, individuals below 2.8m long move into the area with a drop in water temperature below 22°C, and apparently depart for colder Cape Coast waters when temperatures rise above this level, although larger individuals above 2.8m seem to occur there all year round (Compagno, 1984:240). Records suggest that large white sharks have a wide temperature range whereas small sharks (below 3m) may be restricted to temperate seas, suggesting that pupping grounds for the species are also in temperate waters (Carey et.al., 1982:254-260).

Six white sharks were found to have travelled a mean distance of 365 kilometres over an average of 275 days when tagged by South African scientists (Klimley, 1994:132) and it has been suggested that white sharks regulate the timing of their movements so that they arrive at familiar locations at those times of the year when they successfully fed in the past (Klimley, 1994:132). A degree of residency or at least a consistent seasonal movement of the same individuals into the same area has been documented in South Africa (Ferreira and Ferreira 1996) and California (Klimley and Anderson 1996).

11.24 Growth and Reproduction

White sharks have a K selected life history strategy: they are naturally relatively low in abundance, long lived, have relatively low natural mortality and may not reproduce every year. White sharks are poorly adapted to withstand increases in mortality. The majority of females mature between 450 and 500cm length (Francis, 1996) when aged between 12 and 14.5 years old (Klimley, 1994:133) but have been reported as immature at sizes as large as 472cm (Springer, 1939). Males mature at about 350-360cm (Pratt, 1996). Studies of age and growth (Cailliet et al., 1985:49-60, Witner & Cliff, 1998) suggest a generalised age of maturity of 10-12 years.

Since 1980, six pregnant females have been taken from coastal waters off Okinawa in Japan (Uchida *et al.*, 1995), the North Cape, New Zealand (Francis, 1996) and Cape Bon, Tunisia (Fergusson, 1996). Reported litter sizes range from 2-14 foetuses with birth size between 120-160cm length (Fergusson, 1995:36). The reproductive mode is aplacental viviparity with embryos nourished by oophagy and gestation is approximately 12 months. Mating has not been reliably witnessed to date although white sharks are thought to give birth approximately every two years (Klimley, 1994:133). Partuition is thought to occur during the spring and summer in warm-temperate neritic waters where mature adults and neonates occur together as in the shelf waters of the northeastern United States, southern California, southern and eastern Australia, New Zealand, Japan, the Eastern Cape Province of South Africa and the South-Central Mediterranean Sea (Fergusson *et al.* 1996:2). The young are deserted in shallow coastal waters where the risk of falling prey to large sharks and competition for food are low (Fergusson, 1995:36). Fergusson found that the sharks congregate off the western coast of Sicily to mate. The young, which are born around July, are born in a triangle bordered by western Sicily, northern Tunisia and Malta (Nuttall, 1996:8).

Ian Fergusson suggests that Mediterranean sharks classify as a distinct population as they lack a distinctive black oval marking under the front fin that is present in other white sharks. Isolated populations are susceptible to extinction as they can become too small for viable breeding. Extinction of this population would result in a loss of genetic diversity in the species as a whole. Dr Andrew Martin (Colorado University) is carrying out a worldwide collaborative study on white sharks to determine the genetic structure of national populations and the degree of relatedness between populations on a global scale.

11.25 Population Structure

Relatively little is known of the population structures of this species although a regional estimate for the Dangerous Reef population, Southern Australia is given as 200 individuals (Strong et al, 1996). Research suggests that white shark populations may segregate according to size, gender and for reproduction. Strong *et al* (1992) found that the ratio of females to males was 6:1 at Dangerous Reef and other inshore islands off Australia, whereas around the offshore islands of the North and South Neptunes it was 1:20. Strong *et al.* (1992;15-16) found sharks in Spencer Gulf, South Australia (SA) to be segregated by sex and not by size as females were most abundant at 'inshore' islands, whereas males occurred mainly at 'offshore' islands.

Ainley *et.al.,* (1985:109-122) suggested that populations of white sharks are relatively small and difficult to replenish. In a single day in 1982 Micheal McHenry captured 4 adult white sharks near the Farallon Islands following which observations of pinniped white shark attacks decreased by nearly half, taking several years for shark sightings to return to their previous level. The mature population of white sharks in South Africa appears to have been largely destroyed. Sightings or captures of specimens over 500cm are now exceptional and it is unknown how long a full recovery will take (Fergusson *et.al.,* 1996).

In Australia, data sets that have been used to show population declines include beach meshing records for NSW and Queensland, game fishing records from NSW and SA and anecdotal sighting frequencies by ecotourism operators in SA. The data are highly variable and do not take into account environmental fluctuations or changes in catch reporting, fishing practices or levels of fishing effort.

It has been suggested that populations are increasing in some areas (e.g. off central California) as a result of increasing numbers of pinnepeds due to legislation such as the U.S. Marine Mammal Protection Act, 1972 (Miller and Collier, 1980).

In Australia, the National Heritage Trust funds a project involving the Commonwealth Scientific and Industrial Research Organisation (CSIRO), various State and Commonwealth research and management agencies, commercial and recreational fishermen and a number of interested groups which was set up in 1999 to collect information about white sharks in Australian waters which will be used to elucidate and monitor population structures.

11.26 Threats

The main threats to the white shark are recreational and commercial fishing, shark control activities and ecotourism. There is insufficient catch rate data for most of the white sharks' range but big game fishing in California (Klimey, 1985:15-40), Natal (Cliff *et al.* 1989:131-144), the Central Mediterranean Sea (Sicilian Channel) (Fergusson *et al.* 1996:3) and S.E. Australia (Table 11.261) appears to have significantly reduced great white numbers.

Table 11.261 Recreational catch rate data for white sharks in S.E. Australia

YEAR	CATCH RATIO
1960s	1:22
1970s	1:38
1980s	1:651

Source: Pepperell, 1992

However, tag and release amongst gamefishing groups should not be allowed until the effects of this practice upon white sharks has been elucidated. In addition the low-numbers tagged (209 up to September 1999, Bruce 1999) limit the benefit of conventional tagging to examine broad-scale movement patterns. Satellite and archival tags are more effective research measures for white sharks.

Although the white shark has been protected since 1998 the Game Fishing Association of Australia (GFAA) still lists it under their Eligible Species List. Members should be informed of the protected status of the white shark and be able to identify it as small white sharks are often mistaken for other species such as mako sharks. Game fishing organisations must educate their members and national education programmes for commercial and recreational programmes must be instigated.

Even in waters where the white shark is protected they are incidentally caught in commercial fisheries using longlines, hook-and-line, fixed bottom gillnets, fish traps, herring weirs, trammel nets, harpoons, bottom and pelagic trawls and purse seines. These sharks are generally killed to avoid the dangers of handling a live shark. Commercial shark fishermen in Australia have a code of conduct for handling great whites caught incidentally. The white shark is ensnared throughout the water column in nearshore fisheries but is rarely present in the by-catch of offshore oceanic pelagic fisheries (Fergusson *et al.* 1996:2). Fishing gear used by commercial shark fishers has changed since the 1970s. It now includes lighter monofilament polyamide webbing which can be broken by larger sharks, decreased mesh size and raised net height to increase the separation between headline and footline to decrease the possibility of entanglement. However, most catches, other than those from anti-shark nets, are by sport anglers and commercial fishermen that target white sharks in order to trade body parts as trophies. Gordon Hubbell bought a fresh jaw from a 11'10.5" white shark that was caught off Cape Hatteras on May 3 1996 for $500. A similar sized prepared white shark jaw can fetch approximately $7,200 (Hubbell pers.comm). Rarity does not protect species from extinction as the increased financial rewards encourage people to expend greater effort, and break the law, to obtain them.

Incidental captures of white sharks occur in several fisheries worldwide e.g. commercial fisheries in Western Cape, South Africa (Cliff *et al* 1996), New Zealand (Francis 1996), Japan (Uchida *et al* 1996), eastern North Atlantic and Mediterranean Sea (Fergusson 1996). Few fisheries in these areas have requirements to report catches of white sharks making this source of mortality difficult to quantify (EA, 1996a). In Australia the GNO1 (South East Non-Trawl and Southern Shark Fishery) logbook has been modified to specifically mention and record white shark captures and this should be adopted by other white shark regions.

The highest rate of white shark attack is off north-central California averaging 1.3 attacks per year (Miller and Collier, 1981:76-104). Only 0.13 of these attacks per year are fatal compared to the 10 to 20 white sharks killed in this area each year as a by-catch of fisheries (Compagno,1984:241).

498 great white sharks have been captured in beach meshing in NSW between 1950 and 1996. The number of great white sharks caught and

their maximum and average sizes have appeared to decline over time, with an average length of about 2.5m in 1950-70, 2m in 1970-90 and 1.7m in the 1990s. Interannual variability in the capture rates of white sharks in the South African beach meshing program, with a cyclical period of 4-6 years, has been observed (Cliff *et al*, 1996). A beach netting programme should be instigated for satellite or archival tag and release of live sharks and autopsy of dead sharks.

Great white shark cage dives are a big tourist attraction in South Africa and Australia. See Section 5.7 for further details of this practice.

11.27 Protection
The white shark is fully protected in South Africa, Namibia, the Maldives, the US Atlantic, Florida and California and Malta. In Australia it is fully protected under Commonwealth legislation and in the States of Tasmania, South Australia and Victoria. It is commercially protected in Western Australia and protected in New South Wales and Queensland but with exceptions for beach meshing. It is illegal to take great white sharks in NSW with a maximum fine of $20,000 and/or six months in prison (beach meshing contractors excluded). The white shark is listed on the EC Bern Convention with a future listing on the EC Habitats and Species Directive (for further details see Section 9). The white shark is also listed on the UN Barcelona Convention (for

further details see Section 10). Australia have written a draft recovery plan for great white sharks and The Australian Society of Fish Biology list white sharks under 'uncertain status' and are considering a revision to 'vulnerable'

11.28 Future Recommendations

More international protection should be afforded to this wide-ranging species. The great white shark should be listed on CITES Appendix I until more is known about this species and how to manage it.

Research into white shark population dynamics, nursery and mating zones, mortality and life history should be gathered through fisheries log books, public sighting sheets and satellite or archival tag and release of netted sharks that are alive and autopsies on those that are dead. Vulnerable life stage zones must be protected. Cage dive operators can assist research into demography and migration patterns by recording their observations and developing a Code of Conduct that minimises disturbance to the white shark environment. Genetic data should be gathered to distinguish populations. Non-lethal shark control methods should be investigated.

As white shark populations recover so will shark attack rates. It is important to teach people how to minimise their exposure to attack in order to keep public opinion on the side of shark conservation. Where relevant fishermen must be informed of the legal obligation to report capture of great whites and of the illegality of killing the species. Strict penalties must be seen to be enforced to discourage illegal white shark fishing and trade.

12.0 CONCLUSIONS

Sharks are an economically valuable group requiring rational use and conservation. Both individuals and Government bodies must utilise sharks in a sustainable manner and stop assessing sharks solely on their fishery value but recognise the value of sharks in medical and scientific research and shark watching trips. Protection of specific species will benefit other species through habitat protection, reduction of fishery by-catch and maintenance of the marine ecosystem balance. International research must be promoted, particularly genetic studies and appropriate tagging programmes, to elucidate spatial and temporal population trends and to develop population models. Sustainable management plans must be based upon life history information. Research on reproductive rates is being conducted using ultrasound and endoscopes, but these practices are very expensive leaving dissection as the most reliable and viable method. Management plans are a conservation priority. However, scientists show poor use of resources by fishing for dissection specimens when sharks regularly become available through net mortality, by-catch and illegal fishing hauls.

Legislation should be introduced requiring information on commercial and recreational landings and by-catch by species to enable nations to elucidate sustainable catch, if applicable, from known population numbers and recruitment rates. Species identification guides must be produced for this purpose. Information should be gathered on capture area and the length and sex of large shark species. All information should be relayed to the FAO and other global bodies to increase the availability of knowledge to aid other management programmes. Previous logbook data should also be analysed. Legislation should target individual species and different sexes and age classes within that species by applying size limits to catches and returning (or banning) catches of mature females whenever possible. Released sharks should be tagged using an appropriate method and dead sharks autopsied. Shark by-catch should be reduced through use of ITQs and increased selectivity of fishing methods, which will require economic investment in new equipment. It will be necessary to offer economic compensation to the fishermen and impose sanctions on those fishermen who continue to land a high by-catch. Enforcement costs will be high.

Funds are limited such that priority must be given to obtaining legal protection for threatened species and their habitats. National fisheries legislation is necessary to protect sharks because most species frequent coastal areas, particularly mating and nursery zones. Shark aggregation sites should be protected from development and be subject to closed fishing seasons. Protected species status in a few countries may be compromised by unregulated fisheries in other parts of the species' range. Migratory species require international protection which can only be achieved through EC legislation, if the species range is within EC waters, or voluntary conventions. Countries must become members of relevant treaty organisations and existing regimes must be strengthened to reflect the Precautionary Principle.

CITES is limited to international trade, leaving national legislation to regulate takes for local consumption. CITES is vulnerable to corruption from forged permits, collusion between smugglers and government officials, poor enforcement through inadequate financial and human resources, weak penalties and low political support for wildlife conservation. CITES should require that customs monitor trade in certain shark species so that the data collected can form the basis of conservation initiatives. Voluntary conventions like CITES and management plans like IPOA-SHARKS are difficult instruments to enforce. In March 1994 the USA imposed punitive trade sanctions worth $25 million a year on Taiwan for its failure to enforce CITES resolutions but few such penalties are imposed on errant states as few countries can afford to risk upsetting their international relations. Indirect pressure to adhere to conventions and management plans could be brought about by international political bodies. When such bodies assess a potential member country's suitability to join they should consider, amongst other things, the country's record of adherence to the conventions and management plans it has ratified. Maximum attention should be drawn to this area of the selection procedure. Conventions and voluntary management plans have no direct legal force and so it is more fruitful to draw attention to the benefits to be gained from adhering to the instrument than the possible penalties other countries may impose on infringement.

As CITES is species-specific it can do little to control the shark fin trade, as fins are difficult to identify by species. Finning practices can be reduced, irrespective of where the sharks were caught, through national legislation prohibiting the landing of any shark fins unless the shark is landed whole and prohibiting the trade in shark fins. An international convention would encourage less developed countries to participate in the initiative. Human shark protection measures also account for such high shark mortality that research into alternatives is a priority.

Increased public awareness is necessary to persuade authorities to employ measures to protect sharks and to decrease the demand for shark-based consumer products. Non-governmental organisations, recreational fisheries bodies and dive operators should adopt shark education and monitoring programmes, particularly near key population sites. These bodies can act as powerful enforcement tools by reporting illegal activities. Ecotourism activities and the aquarium trade should also be regulated with force of law.

It is beyond the scope of this paper to consider each region, the particular species and fisheries it contains, and the pressures present from ecotourism and shark control measures, and then to apply the above recommendations to the region's particular characteristics. However, consideration of these factors is essential for regional legislative bodies around the globe in order to conserve and manage shark populations.

ANNEXES

Annex 1 Scientific nomenclature for shark species mentioned in this paper

ORDER ORECTOLOBIFORMES – CARPETSHARKS

GINGLYMOSTOMATIDAE	NURSE SHARKS
Ginglymostoma cirratum	Nurse shark
RHINCODONTIDAE	WHALE SHARKS
Rhincodon typus	Whale shark

ORDER HEXANCHIFORMES – SIXGILL, SEVENGILL AND FRILLED SHARKS

HEXANCHIDAE	SIXGILL AND SEVENGILL SHARKS
Hexanchus griseus	Bluntnose sixgill shark
Heptranchias perlo	Sevengill shark
Notorynchus cepedianus	Broadnose or spotted sevengill shark

ORDER SQUALIFORMES – DOGFISH SHARKS

SQUALIDAE	DOGFISH SHARKS
Centrophorus fabricii	Black dogfish
Centrophorus squamosus	Leafscale gulper shark
Centroscymnus coelolepis	Portuguese dogfish
Deania calcea	Birdbeak dogfish
Etmopterus perryi	Dwarf dogfish/lanternshark
Etmopterus princeps	Great lanternshark

Etmopterus pusillus — Smooth lanternshark
Somniosus microcephalus — Greenland sleeper shark
Squalus acanthias — Piked dogfish

ORDER SQUATINIFORMES - ANGELSHARKS

SQUATINIDAE — ANGELSHARKS
Squatina dumeril — Angelshark

ORDER LAMNIFORMES – MACKEREL SHARKS

ALOPIIDAE — THRESHER SHARKS
Alopias pelagicus — Pelagic thresher
Alopias superciliosus — Bigeye thresher
Alopias vulpinus — Thresher shark

CETORHINIDAE — BASKING SHARKS
Cetorhinus maximus — Basking shark

LAMNIDAE — MACKEREL SHARKS
Carcharodon carcharias — Great white shark
Isurus paucus — Longfin mako shark
Isurus oxyrinchus — Shortfin mako
Lamna nasus — Porbeagle
Odontaspis noronhai — Bigeye sand tiger

MEGACHASMIDAE — MEGAMOUTH SHARKS
Megachasma pelagios — Megamouth shark

ODONTASPIDAE	SAND TIGER SHARKS
Eugomphodus taurus	Sand tiger, spotted raggedtooth or grey nurse
Odontaspis ferox	Smalltooth sand tiger

ORDER CARCHARHINIFORMES – GROUND SHARKS

CARCHARHINIDAE	REQUIEM SHARKS
Carcharhinus albimarginatus	Silvertip shark
Carcharhinus altimus	Bignose shark
Carcharhinus amblyrhynchos	Grey reef shark
Carcharhinus brachyurus	Copper shark
Carcharhinus brevipinna	Spinner shark
Carcharhinus dussumieri	Whitecheek shark
Carcharhinus falciformis	Narrowtooth/Silky shark
Carcharhinus fitzroyensis	Creek whaler
Carcharhinus galapagensis	Galapagos shark
Carcharhinus leucas	Bull shark
Carcharhinus limbatus	Blacktip shark
Carcharhinus longimanus	Oceanic whitetip shark
Carcharhinus melanopterus	Blacktip reef shark
Carcharhinus obscurus	Dusky shark
Carcharhinus perezi	Reef shark
Carcharhinus plumbeus	Sandbar shark
Carcharhinus sorrah	Spot-tail shark
Carcharhinus taurus	Sand tiger shark
Galeocerdo cuvier	Tiger shark

Glyphis gangeticus	Ganges shark
Negaprion brevirostris	Lemon shark
Prionace glauca	Blue shark
Rhizoprionodon acutus	Milk shark
Rhizoprionodon porosus	Caribbean sharpnose
Rhizoprionodon terraenovae	Atlantic sharpnose
Triaenodon obesus	Whitetip reef shark

SCYLIORHINIDAE	CATSHARKS
Scyliorhinus canicula	Small-spotted catshark

SPHYRNIDAE	HAMMERHEAD SHARKS
Sphyrna lewini	Scalloped hammerhead
Sphyrna mokarran	Great hammerhead
Sphyrna tiburo	Bonnethead shark
Sphyrna zygaena	Smooth hammerhead

TRIAKIDAE	HOUNDSHARKS
Galeorhinus galeus	Tope/Soupfin shark
Mustelus antarcticus	Gummy shark
Mustelus henlei	Brown smooth-hound
Mustelus lenticulatus	Spotted estuary smooth-hound
Triakis semifasciata	Leopard shark

Annex 2 Fishing Methods
(Nédéléc, 1990)

Gillnets Panels of mesh in which fish become entangled. Gillnets may be floated at the surface and allowed to drift, or fixed to the bottom or in midwater. Gillnets are indiscriminate in what they catch.

Longlines One main line to which shorter lines with baited or unbaited hooks are attached at fixed intervals. Floats may be attached to the main line allowing the gear to float.

Purse seines Catch fish by surrounding them from the sides and from beneath. A long panel of net is let from a catcher vessel and drawn in a circle by a skiff. Once the circle is closed, a line along the bottom of the net draws the net closed and the net is brought on board with the help of a power-block.

Trawl A funnel-shaped fishing net towed behind a vessel, that is effective for catching fish on or near the sea floor.

Set nets A gillnet suspended vertically from floats at fixed locations to target migratory fish.

Annex 3 Fishery bodies

Asia Pacific Economic Cooperation (APEC)

APEC was established in 1989 to promote open trade and economic cooperation among economies around the Pacific Rim, and, under APEC, the Fisheries Working Group (FWG) was formed in 1991. The FWG meets annually, and deliberates on a broad range of living marine resource issues and specific project proposals. The 21 APEC Economies are invited to these FWG meetings. In recent years, the FWG has concentrated in the areas of management; trade and marketing; seafood inspection training; aquaculture; and various environmental issues.

In addition, a special ad hoc workshop on fisheries management was held in Kesennuma City, Japan, in July 1999.

Indian Ocean Tuna Commission (IOTC)

The IOTC came into force in March 1996. Within FAO Statistical Areas 51 and 57, the IOTC promotes cooperation among members regarding appropriate management, conservation, and optimum utilization of the following species: Yellowfin tuna (*Thunnus albacares*), Skipjack tuna (*Katsuwonus pelamis*), Bigeye tuna (*Thunnus obesus*), Albacore (*Thunnus alalunga*), Southern Bluefin tuna (*Thunnus maccoyii*), Longtail tuna (*Thunnus tonggol*), Kawakawa (*Euthynnus affinis*), Frigate tuna (*Auxis thazard*), Bullet tuna (*Auxis rochei*), Narrow-barred Spanish Mackerel (*Scomberomorus concolor*), Indo-Pacific King Mackerel (*Scomberomorus guttatus*), Indo-Pacific Blue Marlin (*Makaira mazara*), Black Marlin (*Makaira indica*), Striped Marlin (*Tetrapturus audax*), Indo-Pacific Sailfish (*Istiophorus platypterus*) and Swordfish (*Xiphias gladius*). The IOTC is open to members of FAO that are coastal States, are responsible for international relations of territories in the area, or regularly engage in fishing in the area, as well as regional economic integration organisations. Upon approval, other members of the United Nations may become members if they engage in fishing in the area.

International Convention for the Conservation of Atlantic Tunas (ICCAT)

ICCAT was established to provide an effective program of international cooperation in research and conservation in recognition of the unique problems related to the highly migratory nature of tunas and tuna-like species. The Convention area is defined as all waters of the Atlantic Ocean, including the adjacent seas. The Commission is responsible for providing internationally coordinated research on the condition of the Atlantic tunas and tuna-like species, and their environment, as well as for the development of regulatory recommendations. The objective of such regulatory recommendations is to conserve and manage species of tuna and tuna-like species throughout their range in a manner that maintains their population at levels that will permit the maximum sustainable catch.

International Council for the Exploration of the Sea (ICES)

ICES is the oldest oceanographic organization in the North Atlantic area and is the premier body for giving advice at the international level on scientific and policy matters relating to fisheries, pollution and other marine environmental issues. ICES provides advice on pollution matters to the London, Oslo and Helsinki Conventions for Marine Pollution, and on fisheries matters to the Convention for the Conservation of Salmon in the North Atlantic Ocean (NASCO); the United States is a party to all of these conventions. ICES also advises the North-East Atlantic Fisheries Commission (NEAFC) and the International Baltic Sea Fishery Commission. ICES also has strong formal ties to the Intergovernmental Oceanographic Commission (IOC), to which the United States belongs, and the annual ICES meeting is the major forum for coordinating the planning and execution of ICES/IOC joint research on living marine resources in the North Atlantic.

Inter-American Tropical Tuna Commission (IATTC)

The IATTC was established to "(1) study the biology of the tunas and related species of the eastern Pacific Ocean with a view to determining the effects that fishing and natural factors have on their abundance, and (2) to recommend appropriate conservation measures so that the stocks of fish can be maintained at levels which will afford maximum sustainable catches." The Commission's duties were broadened in 1976 to include work on the problems arising from the tuna-dolphin relationship in the eastern Pacific Ocean.

Latin American Organisation for Fishery Development (OLDEPESCA)

The members of OLDEPESCA are States belonging to the Latin American Economic System which have ratified the Agreement. The main purpose of the Organization is to meet Latin American food requirements adequately, making use of Latin American fishery resource potential for the benefit of Latin American peoples, by concerted action in promoting the constant development of the countries and the permanent strengthening of regional cooperation in this sector. To this end, the objectives of OLDEPESCA are as follows:

    a. To promote adequate utilization of fishery resources, preserving the marine and freshwater environment through the application of rational policies for the conservation of resources.

b. To encourage and strengthen Latin American cooperation in the development of the rational exploitation of sea and freshwater fishery resources, for the benefit of the peoples in the region.

c. To increase substantially a food supply of sufficient nutritional value, the prices, preparation and presentation of which are in keeping with the needs of the low-income inhabitants of the region.

d. To increase consumption of marine and freshwater products in the region.

e. To encourage export diversification and expansion.

f. To promote marketing systems to expand the regional exchange of products of the sector.

g. To promote generation of jobs and improvement of incomes, through greater social and economic development of the communities related to the fish of the region.

h. To improve and strengthen the productive, institutional, organizational and human resources capacity of the sector.

i. To promote and organize utilization of the joint negotiating capacity of the Latin American region, as well as to determine, identify and channel international, technical and financial cooperation, through concrete regional coordination and cooperation within the scope of the sector.

Multilateral High Level Conference (MHLC)

The MHLC is a series of conference negotiations striving to design and implement a conservation and management regime for highly migratory fish stocks in the western and central Pacific Ocean. There have been five MHLC meetings to date, with a sixth planned in Honolulu in April 2000. Participation in this process has grown to include representatives of Australia, Chinese Taipei, the Cook Islands, the Federated States of Micronesia, Fiji, France, French Polynesia, Indonesia, Japan, Kirabati, the Marshall Islands, Nauru, New Caledonia, New Zealand, Niue, Palau, Papua New Guinea, People's Republic of China, Philippines, Republic of Korea, Samoa, the Solomon Islands, Tonga, Tuvalu, United States, Vanuatu, and Wallis and Futuna.

MHLC2, held in Majuro, Marshall Islands, June 10-13, 1997, set an agenda and defined success for the process. It adopted by acclamation the Majuro Declaration which expresses the commitment of the participants to negotiate, over a 3-year period, a legally binding conservation and management regime for western and central Pacific highly migratory fish stocks. These stocks support fisheries that produce over 50 percent of the world's tuna catch, and are thus probably the largest and most valuable that are not yet subject to a conservation and management regime. Fortunately, of the tuna stocks likely to be covered, all are believed to be in healthy condition, with the possible exception of bigeye tuna. Achieving the stated goal may be what was called the most significant potential development in that part of the world, given the importance of fish resources to many Pacific island economies.

Northwest Atlantic Fisheries Organization (NAFO)

NAFO is the successor organization to the International Commission for the Northwest Atlantic Fisheries (ICNAF). Its mission is: (1) to provide for continued multilateral consultation and cooperation with respect to the study, appraisal, and exchange of scientific information and views relating to fisheries of the Convention Area and (2) to conserve and manage fishery resources of the Regulatory Area, i.e., that part of the Convention Area which lies beyond the areas in which coastal states exercise fisheries jurisdiction. The Convention Area is located within the waters of the Northwest Atlantic ocean roughly north of 35° north latitude and west of 42° west latitude. (Note: The Convention applies to all fishery resources of the Convention Area with the exception of: salmon; tunas, swordfish, and marlins; cetacean stocks managed by the International Whaling Commission or any successor organization; and sedentary species of the Continental Shelf.)

In Sept 1998 NAFO adopted recommendations calling for improved training and identification and reporting in elasmobranchs and swift assessment of elasmobranchs in the NAFO Regulatory Area in response to the CITES resolution on shark data collection.

For further information on fishery bodies see Marashi 1996.

For further information on international fisheries management see Weber & Fordham 1996.

Annex 4 Useful Website Addresses

American Elasmobranch Society
www.elasmo.org

Asia Shark Watch
www.asiaticmarine.com

Environment Australia
www.ea.gov.au

European Commission
www.europa.eu.int

Food and Agriculture Organisation
www.fao.org

Fox Shark Research Foundation
www.rodneyfox.com.au

National Audubon Society
www.audubon.org

SeaWeb
www.seaweb.org

Shark Trust
www.sharktrust.org

Shark Specialist Group
www.flmnh.ufl.edu/fish/research/iucn

TRAFFIC
www.traffic.org

UK CITES
www.ukcites.gov.uk

UK Department for Environment, Transport and the Regions
www.detr.gov.uk

UK Ministry of Agriculture Fisheries and Food
	www.maff.gov.uk

United Nations
	www.un.org

United Nations Environment Program
	www.unep.ch

National Marine Fisheries Service
	www.nmfs.noaa.gov

World Conservation Monitoring Centre
	www.wcmc.org

World Wildlife Fund
	www.wwf-uk.org

REFERENCES

Ainley, D.G., C.S. Strong, H.R. Huber, T.J. Lewis and S.H. Morrell (1981) "Predation by sharks on pinnepeds at the Farallon Islands". Fish.Bull.NOAA/NMFS, 78:941-5.

Ainley, D.G., R.P. Henderson, H.R. Huber, R.J. Boekelheide, S.G. Allen, and T.L. McElroy (1985) "Dynamics of White Shark/Pinniped Interactions in the Gulf of the Farallones". Memoirs of the Southern California Academy of Sciences, 9:109-22.

Ames, J.A. and G.V. Morejohn, (1980)"Evidence of white shark, *Carcharodon carcharias,* attacks on sea otters, *Enhydra lutris*". Calif. Fish Game, 66(4):196-209.

Anderson, E.D. (1990) "Fishery models as applied to elasmobranch fisheries" In H.L. Pratt Jr., S.H.Gruber, and T. Taniuchi (eds) Elasmobranchs as living resources: advances in the biology, ecology, systematics, and the status of the fisheries, United States Department of Commerce, NOAA Technical Report NMFS 90:473-484.

Anderson, R.C. and H. Ahmed (1993) "Shark fisheries in the Maldives", Ministry of Fisheries and Agriculture, Male,

Republic of Maldives, and Food and Agriculture Organisation of the United Nations, 76pp.

Anderson, R.C. and M.H. Maniku (1996) "Conservation of chondrichthyans in the Maldives", Shark News, Issue 7, June 1996:14.

Anon, (1976) "El Tiburon: Mas Benefico que Terrible" Tecnica Pesquera, No. 99.

Anon, (1986) "Sharks Get Protection: Put-em-back alive code for Anglers" Angler's Mail April 12th.

Anon (1987) "Permanece Anclado el *Tiburon V* en Tampico Por Falta de Cuidados" Tecnica Pesquera, no 233.

Anon, (1989) "Report to the Southern Shark Fishery Management Advisory Committee" Southern Shark Assessment Workshop 5, Queenscliff, Australia : Marine Research Laboratories.

Anon (1989b) Report of the Study Group on Elasmobranch Fisheries, ICES CM 1989/G:54. International Council for Exploration of the Seas, Copenhagen, Denmark.

Anon (1990) "Ocean Predator is Preyed Upon: Sharks need help, Officials say" The New York Times 8th May, 1990.

Anon (1990b) "Eye to Eye with the Great White Shark", Calypso Log, December 1990:6-7.

Anon (1991) "Mass Murder", Politiken, Denmark November 11, 1991.

Anon (1991b) "Elasmobranch Conservation: the establishment of the IUCN shark specialist group", Aquatic Conservation, 1, 193 -194).

Anon. (1991c) "Fishery management plan for sharks of the Atlantic Ocean". US Dept of Commerce, NOAA, Southeast Regional Office, St Petersburg, Florida. Pp 1-147.

Anon. (1991d) "1989 Yearbook of Fisheries Statistics. Vol 69. Catches and Landings" (FAO:Rome) 516pp.

Anon. (1993) Fishery management plan for sharks of the Atlantic Ocean US Department of Commerce, NOAA, South-East Regional Office, St. Petersburg, FL. 167pp + Appendices.

Anon (1993b) Deep Sea Angling Logbook Statistics 1978-92 Central Fisheries Board, Mobhi Boreen, Glasnevin, Dublin 9, Ireland.

Anon. (1994) Report of the shark evaluation workshop, March 14-18, 1994 NOAA, NMFS, Southeast Fishery Center, Miami: 47pp.

Anon (1994b) IUCN red list categories, IUCN Species Survival Commission, Gland, Switzerland: 13pp.

Anon. (1994c) Biodiversity. The UK action plan London, HMSO for Department of the Environment (Cm.2428.)

Anon. (1994d) "Regional News: Canada" Shark News, Issue 1, June 1994:7.

Anon (1994e) East Coast Tuna and Billfish Fishery, 1994, Fisheries Assessment Report. East Coast Tuna and Billfish Fishery Assessment Group (Comp.)

Anon (1994f) Guidelines for Protected Area Management Categories. Commission on National Parks and Protected Areas with the assistance of the World Conservation Monitoring Centre, Gland, Switzerland.

Anon. (1995) 1995 Atlantic Management Plan: Porbeagle, Shortfin Mako and Blue Sharks. Canada: Department of Fisheries and Oceans.

Anon. (1995b) Biodiversity: The UK Steering Group Report, London, HMSO for Department of the Environment.

Anon. (1995c) Marine Scene, Issue No.2, January 1993. Peterborough, UK: Joint Nature Conservation Committee.

Anon. (1995d) Marine Scene, Issue No.6, Winter 1995/6. Peterborough, UK: Joint Nature Conservation Committee.

Anon. (1995e) Marine Information Notes, Number 2, edition 3, June 1995. Peterborough, UK: Joint Nature Conservation Committee.

Anon. (1995f) Marine Information Notes, Number 3, edition 1, June 1995. Peterborough, UK: Joint Nature Conservation Committee.

Anon (1995g) "Basking sharks attacked by man" Press release, Marine Conservation Society, 19 May 1995.

Anon. (1996a) "Shark!" Biodiversity Legal Foundation leaflet, Colorado, USA.

Anon (1996b) "Written Answers to Questions", Hansard issue 1727:503 - 505 and 557-558.

Anon (1996c) "Facts about the shark fin trade" Shark Protection League Information Sheet, London, England.

Anon (1996d) "Marine Fish and the IUCN Red List of Threatened Animals" In E.Hudson and G. Mace (eds). Report of the workshop held in collaboration with WWF and IUCN at the Zoological Society of London from April 29th May 1st, 1996.

Anon (1996e) "School Shark Stock Assessment, April 1996" Report to the Southern Shark Fishery Management Advisory Committee (SharkMAC) from the Southern Shark Fishery Assessment Group (SharkFAG), April 1996, Australia: SharkFAG.

Anon (1996f) DRAFT Discussion Paper Pursuant to CITES Resolution Conf. 9.17 -An overview of the biological status of Shark species Maryland, USA: National Marine Fisheries Service.

Anon (1996g) 1996 Report of the Shark Evaluation Workshop, June 1996. FL,USA: NOAA National Marine Fisheries Service.

Anon (1996h) Shark News! Newsletter of the white shark research institute. Issue 7:2.

Anon (1996i) "UN Press Release GA/9192".

Anon (1998). Managing the Nation's By-catch: Programs, Activities, and Recommendations for the National Marine Fisheries

Service. NOAA, U.S.Department of Commerce, Washington, D.C. 174 pp.

Anon (1998b) "Sharks on the Line" Ocean Wildlife Campaign.

Anon (1998c) "White shark exploitation in South Africa" Shark News 12, November 1998.

Anon (1999a). Final Fishery Management Plan for Atlantic Tuna, Swordfish, and Sharks. NOAA/NMFS, U.S. Department of Commerce, April, 1999.

Anon (1999b). Fisheries of the United States, 1998. NOAA/NMFS, U.S. Department of Commerce, July,1999.

Anon (1999c). DRAFT. Environmental assessment/regulatory impact review/initial regulatory flexibility analysis for amendments 63/63 to the fishery management plans for the groundfish fisheries of the Bering Sea/Aleutian Islands and Gulf of Alaska to revise management of sharks and skates. Prepared April 2, 1999, by the North Pacific Fishery Management Council and Alaska Dept. of Fish and Game, Juneau, AK. 72 pp.

Anon (2000a) "Draft recovery plan for Great White Sharks in Australia" Environment Australia 2000, Canberra.

Anon (2000b) "Draft recovery plan for Grey Nurse Sharks in Australia" Environment Australia 2000, Canberra.

Anon (2000c) "Commissioner FISCHLER calls for measures to conserve deep-water species" European Commission Press Release (06/07/2000)

Anon (2000d) "FISCHLER launches discussion on the future of the Common Fisheries Policy" European Commission Press Release (28/06/2000)

Anon (2000e) "Draft United States National Plan of Action for the Conservation and Management of Sharks", NOAA/NMFS, U.S. Department of Commerce July 2000.

Anon (2000f) Ovarian Cancer Research Notebook (www.slip.net/~mcdavis)

Anon (2000g) "Bad news from Thailand for Whale Sharks" Shark Focus Issue 8 July 2000.

Anon (2000h) "Booming Trade Threatens World's Shark Populations" World Wildlife Fund website www.wwf-uk.org/news/sharks

ANZECC (1998) Guidelines for Establishing the National Representative System of Marine Protected Areas. Australian and New Zealand Environment and Conservation Council, Task Force on Marine Protected Areas. Environment Australia, Canberra.

Arnold, P.W. (1972) "Predation on the harbour porpoise, *Phocoena phocoena* by a white shark, *Carcharodon carcharias*", J. Fish. Res. Board Can., 29:1213-4.

Babbitt, B (1994) "Sharks: the killing game", Tide, May/June 1994:7-20.

Baldridge, H.D. Jr. (1972) "Accumulation and function of liver oil in Florida sharks" Copeia, 1972:306-324.

Baldridge, H.D. Jr., and J. Williams (1969) "Shark attack: feeding or fighting?" Milit. Med., 134(2):130-133.

Bass, A.J. (1978) "Problems in studies of sharks in the southwest Indian Ocean" In E.S. Hodgson & R.F.Mathewson (eds.) Sensory Biology of Sharks, Skates and Rays, Office of Naval Research, Department of the Navy, Arlington, pp. 545-594.

Bedford, D (1987) "Shark management: a case history - the California pelagic shark and swordfish fishery" In S. Cook (ed) <u>Sharks: an inquiry into biology, behavior, fisheries, and use</u>, Oregon State University Sea Grant Publication, Corvallis, Oregon : 161-171.

Berrow, S.D. (1994) "Incidental capture of elasmobranchs in the bottom set gill-net fishery off the south coast of Ireland" <u>J. Mar. Biol. Ass. UK,</u> 74: 837-847.

Berrow, S.D. and C. Heardman (1994) "The basking shark *Cetorhinus maximus* (Gunnerus) in Irish waters - patterns of distribution and abundance". <u>Proc. Roy. Irish Acad. 94B</u>, 2. 101-107.

Bigelow, H.B. and W.C. Schroeder (1948) "Sharks". <u>Mem.Sears Found. Mar. Res.,</u>(1):53-576.

Bigelow, H.B., Farfante, I.P., and Schroeder, W.C. (1948) "Fishes of the western North Atlantic" <u>Memoir Sears Foundation for Marine Research,</u> 1 (1), 576pp.

Blaber, S.J.M. (1986) "Feeding selectivity of a guild of piscivorous fish in mangrove areas of north-west Australia" <u>Aust.J.Mar.Freshwater Res.</u> 37:329-336.

Blaber, S.J.M., J.W. Young and M.C. Dunning (1985) "Community structure and zoogeographic affinities of the coastal fishes of the Dampier region of north-western Australia" Aust.J.Mar.Freshwater Res. 36:247-266.

Blaber, S.J.M., D.T. Brewer, and J.P. Salini (1989) "Species composition and biomass of fishes in different habitats of a tropical northern Australian estuary: their occurrence in the adjoining sea and estuarine dependence," Estuarine, Coastal and Shelf Science, 29:509-531

Blenchley, P (1974) Jaws, New York : Doubleday.

Bonfil, R (1994) "Overview of world elasmobranch fisheries" FAO Fisheries Technical Paper No.341. Rome: FAO, 119p.

Branstetter, S (1980) "Shark Early Life History - One Reason Sharks Are Vulnerable to Overfishing" In S.H. Gruber (ed) Discovering Sharks, Special Publication No.14 of the American Littoral Society pages 29-34.

Bright, M (1987) "Basking sharks", BBC Wildlife Magazine, August 1987, pp407-409.

Briggs, J.C. (1960) "Fishes of worldwide (circumtropical) distribution". Copeia, 1960, 171-180.

Bruce,B (1989) "Biology of the White Shark", SAFISH, 14 (1):4-7.

Bruce, B (1999) "Game-fish tag-release of white sharks – an issues paper for the National White Shark Research Working Group" CSIRO Marine Research.

Bruce, B.D. (1991) "Preliminary Observations on the Biology of the White Shark, *Carcharodon carcharias,* in South Australian waters", Australian Journal of Marine and Freshwater Research, Vol 43, No 1 pp 1-11.

Budker, P (1971) The life of sharks. New York : Columbia University Press.

Burgess, G.H. (1980) "Shark Attack and the International Shark Attack File" In S.H.Gruber (ed) Discovering Sharks, Special Publication No.14 of the American Littoral Society pages 101-105.

Burgess, G.H. and M. Callahan (1996) "Worldwide Patterns of White Shark Attacks on Humans", International Shark Attack File, Florida Museum of Natural History.

Cailliet, G.M. (1990) "Elasmobranch age determination and verification: an updated review" In H.L. Pratt Jr., S.H.Gruber, and T. Taniuchi (eds) <u>Elasmobranchs as living resources: advances in the biology, ecology, systematics, and the status of the fisheries,</u> United States Department of Commerce, NOAA Technical Report NMFS 90:157-65.

Cailliet, G.M. (1992) "Demography of the central California population of the leopard shark (*Triakis1 semifasciata*)" <u>Aust. Journal of Marine and Freshwater Research,</u> vol 43, no 1 pp183-93.

Cailliet, G.M., D.B. Holts and D. Bedford (1992) "Review of the commercial fisheries for sharks on the west coast of the United States" <u>Proceedings of the American Elasmobranch Society Annual Meeting, New York, 1991.</u>

Cailliet, G.M., H.F. Mollet, G.G. Pittenger, D. Bedford and L.J. Natanson (1992) "Growth and demography of the Pacific Angel shark (*Squatina californica),* based upon tag returns off California" <u>Australian Journal of Marine and Freshwater Research,</u> 43, No 1.

Camhi, M (1995) "Galapagos under siege", Shark News, Issue 5, October 1995:10.

Camhi, M (1999) " Sharks on the Line II: An analysis of Pacific State Shark Fisheries" Living Oceans Program, National Audubon Society.

Campbell D., Battaglene T and W. Shafron (1992) "Economics of resource conservation in a commercial shark fishery" Australian Journal of Marine and Freshwater Research, Vol 43, No 1 pp 251-62.

Carey, F.G., J.W. Kanwisher, O. Brazier, G. Gabrielson, J.G. Casey and H.L. Pratt Jr. (1982) "Temperature and activities of a white shark, *Carcharodon*".Copeia, (2):254-60.

Carrier, J.C. (1996) "Identification and closure of nurse shark breeding grounds", Shark News, March 1996:6.

Carrier, J.C. and C.A. Luer (1990) "Growth rates in the nurse shark, *Ginglymostoma cirratum*", Copeia, 3:686-692.

Carrier, J.C., H.L. Pratt Jr and L.K. Martin (1994) "Group Reproductive Behaviors in Free-Living Nurse Sharks, *Ginglymostoma cirratum,*" Copeia, 3:646 -656.

Casey, J.G. and N.E. Kohler (1980) "Long distance movements of Atlantic Sharks from the NMFS Cooperative Shark Tagging Program" In S.H. Gruber (ed)Discovering Sharks, Special Publication No.14 of the American Littoral Society pages 87 -91.

Casey, J.G. and N.E. Kohler (1992) "Tagging studies on the shortfin mako shark (*Isurus oxyrinchus*) in the western North Atlantic" Aust. Journal of Marine and Freshwater Research, vol 43, no 1 pp45-60.

Casey, J.G., and H.L. Pratt (1985) "Distribution of the White Shark, *Carcharodon carcharias,* in the Western North Atlantic". Memoirs of the Southern California Academy of Sciences 9:2 -14.

Castillo Geniz, J.L. (1991) "Tiburon", Panorama Pesquero 1(3).

Castro, J.I. (1993) A field guide to the sharks commonly caught in commercial fisheries of the southeastern United States NOAA Technical Memorandum, NMFS-SEFSC-338. America : National Oceanic and Atmospheric Administration.

Castro, J.I. (1996) <u>Status of overexploited shark species: an analysis of FAO shark landings data, CITES replies, and IUCN Reports.</u> USA: NOAA.

Caughley, G (1977) <u>Analysis of Vertebrate Populations</u> Wiley: New York.

Chan, Z (2000) "Author Peter Benchley spearheads fight to save the much maligned fish from extinction" <u>South China Morning Post</u> 5, August 2000.

Cherry, M (1991) "Saving the Shark", <u>Nature,</u> vol 350, issue 6320, page 645.

Che-Tsung, C, Kwang-Ming L and Shoou-Jeng J (1997) "Preliminary report on Taiwan's Whale Shark Fishery" <u>Traffic Bulletin,</u> Vol. 17 (1), September 1997.

Clark, E. (1963) <u>The Lady and the Sharks.</u> New York: Harper & Row.

Clark, E and von Schmidt, K (1965) "Sharks of the central Gulf coast of Florida" <u>Bulletin of Marine Science</u> 15, 13-83.

Clemens, W.A. and G.V. Wilby (1961) "Fishes of the Pacific coast of Canada". <u>Fisheries Research Board of Canada</u>, Bulletin 86, 2nd ed.

Cliff, G. (1991) "Trends in the catch rates of large sharks in the Natal meshing program". Proceedings of Conservation Workshop, Sharks Down Under Conference, Sydney. Taronga Zoo: Sydney.

Cliff, G., Dudley, S.F.J. and Davis, B (1988) "An overview of shark catches in Natal's shark nets: 1966 to1986" South African National Scientific Programmes Report No. 157.

Cliff, G., S.F.J. Dudley, and B. Davis (1989) "Sharks Caught in the Protective Gill Nets off Natal, South Africa. 2. The Great White Shark *Carcharodon carcharias* (Linnaeus)". South African Journal of Marine Science 8:131-44.

Cliff G, Van Der Elst, RP, Govender A, Witthun TK and Bullen EM (1996) First estimates of mortality and population size of white sharks on the South African coast. In AP Klimley and D Ainley (eds) Great white sharks: the biology of *Carcharodon carcharias.* Pp 393-400 Academic Press, San Diego.

Collier, R.S. (1964) "Report on a recent shark attack off San Francisco, California", California Fish and Game volume 50 no.4:261 -264.

Collier, R.S. (1992) "Recurring attacks by white sharks on divers at two Pacific sites off Mexico and California", <u>Environmental Biology of Fishes,</u> 33:319-325.

Collier, R.S. (1993) "Shark Attacks off the California Islands: Review and Update" In F.G. Hochberg (ed) <u>Third California Islands Symposium: Recent Advances in Research on the California Islands.</u> Santa Barbara, CA: Santa Barbara Museum of Natural History. Pg 453-462.

Compagno, L.J.V. (1984) <u>FAO Species Catalogue. Vol. 4. Sharks of the World : An Annotated and Illustrated Catalogue of Shark Species Known to Date. Part 1. Hexanchiformes to Lamniformes.</u> FAO Fish. Synop., (125) Vol.4, Pt.1:249p. Rome: Food and Agriculture Organization of the United Nations.

Compagno, L.J.V. (1984) <u>FAO Species Catalogue. Vol. 4. Sharks of the World : An Annotated and Illustrated Catalogue of Shark Species Known to Date. Part 2. Carcharhiniformes.</u> FAO Fish. Synop., (125) Vol.4, Pt.2: 251-655.Rome : Food and Agriculture Organization of the United Nations.

Compagno, L.J.V. (1990) "Shark exploitation and conservation",

NOAA Tech. Report. NMFS 90, 391-414.

Compagno, L.J.V. (1991) "Government Protection for the great white shark (*Carcharodon carcharias*) in South Africa", South African Journal of Science, vol 87:284-285.

Compagno, L.J.V. and S.F. Cook (1995) "Freshwater elasmobranchs: a questionable future", Shark News, March 1995:4-5.

Cook, S.F. (1990) "Trends in shark fin markets: 1980, 1990, and beyond" Chondros, 15 March 1990:3-6.

Cook, S.F. (1995) "Cyanide spill in the Essequibo River, Guyana", Shark News, Issue 5, October 1995:10.

Cook, S.F. (1996) "Spiny dogfish landings crash in British Columbia", Shark News, Issue 7, June 1996:12-13.

Coppleson, V.M. (1962) Shark attack, 2nd edition, Sydney: Angus and Robertson.

Cortes, E. (1999a). Standardized diet compositions and trophic levels of sharks. ICES Journal of Marine Science 56:707-717.

Cortes, E. (1999b). "A stochastic stage-based population model of the sandbar shark in the western North Atlantic". In: Life in the slow lane: ecology and conservation of long-lived marine animals. J.A. Musick editor, American Fisheries Society Symposium 23, Bethesda, MD Pp 115-136.

Cortes, E. (1999c). 1999 Shark Evaluation Annual Report. Document SFD-98/99-64. July, 1999. NMFS Southeast Fisheries Science Center, Panama City Florida

Davies, D.H. (1964) About sharks and shark attack, Durban: Brown, Davis and Platt.

Davis, C. (1983) "The awesome basking shark", Sea Front., 29(2):78-85.

Dayton, L (1991) "Save the sharks", New Scientist, vol 130 (1773), p34 -37.

DG Fisheries, (pers comm.), Artur Payer (00-32-2-2996666)

DG Statistics (pers comm.) David Cross (00-35-2-430137249)

Dockerty, T. (1995) International Trade in Shark Fins, Cambridge, England: Wildlife Trade Monitoring Unit.

Dold, C (1996) "Shark Therapy" Discover, April 1996:51-57.

Dudley, S (1993) "Shark control measures: the Natal Sharks Board and shark conservation" Shark News, Issue 4, July 1995:1-2

Dudley, S.F.J. and G. Cliff (1993) "Some effects of shark nets in the Natal nearshore environment", Environmental Biology of Fishes, 36:243-255.

Dulvy, N (pers.comm) School of Biological Sciences, University of East Anglia, Norwich NR4 7TJ. Telephone (01603) 456161.

Eckersley, Y (1996) "Shark meshing is the net result justifiable? GEO Australia 18(5):17-26.

Ellis, R. (1995) Monsters of the Sea. London : Robert Hale.

Ellis, R., and J.E. McCosker (1991) Great White Shark. New York: Stanford University Press.

English Nature (pers.comm.) Paul Knapman 01733-455229

Eno, C (1991) "3.6 Shark Fisheries: Basking sharks, blue sharks and porbeagles" Marine Conservation Handbook, Nature Conservancy Council: Peterborough.

Fahy, E and P. Gleeson (1989) The post-peak gill-net fishery for Spurdog, *Squalus acanthias* L.in Western Ireland. Department of the Marine, Ireland. Irish Fisheries Investigations, Series B (Marine) 35.

Farquhar, G.B. (1963) "Sharks of the family Lamnidae", Tech.Rep.U.S.Navy Oceanogr.Off., (TR-157):22p.

Fergusson, I.K. (1996) "Report on the distribution & autecology of the white shark *Carcharodon carcharias* in the North-Eastern Atlantic and Mediterranean Sea", In A.P. Klimley & D.G. Ainley, (eds) <u>Great White Sharks: Ecology & Behaviour.</u> Orlando : Academic Press.

Fergusson, I.K. (1995) "Great white lies", <u>BBC Wildlife,</u> vol.13, no.4, April 1995 pp32-37.

Fergusson, I.K. and L.J.V. Compagno (1994) "IICES: The International Initiative for Conservation of White Sharks", <u>Shark News</u> Issue 1, June 1994:3.

Fergusson, I.K., L.J.V. Compagno, and M.A. Marks (1996) <u>IUCN Reference : Coastal-Pelagic Elasmobranch Species Accounts</u> : IUCN.

Fergusson, I.K., L.J.V. Compagno, and M.A. Marks (1996) IUCN Category Review for Great White Sharks : IUCN.

Ferreira, C. (pers.comm.) White Shark Research Institute, PO Box 50775, V&A Waterfront, Cape Town, South Africa 8001. Tel. (021) 9052426 Fax. (021) 5511632

Ferreira CA and Ferreira TP (1996) "Population dynamics of white sharks in South Africa. In: <u>Great white sharks. The biology of</u>

Carcharodon carcharias. AP Klimley & DG Ainley eds. Academic Press, New York NY USA Pp 381-391.

Fleming, E.H and Papageorgiou P.A (1997) "Shark Fisheries and Trade in Europe" TRAFFIC Europe 78pp

Fowler, S.L. (pers. comm) – 01635-550380

Fowler, S.L. (1996) IUCN Category Review for Basking Sharks: IUCN.

Fowler, S.L. and Earll, R.C. (1994) (eds) Proceedings of the second European Shark and Ray Workshop, 15-16 February 1994: Tag and release schemes and shark and ray management plans. Unpublished report. 57pp.

Francis, M.P. (1996) "Observations on a pregnant female white shark (*Carcharodon carcharias*), with a review of reproduction in the species". In A.P. Klimley & D.G. Ainley (eds) Great White Sharks : Ecology and Behaviour : Orlando, Academic Press.

Freestone, D (1991) "The Precautionary Principle" in R.R. Churchill and D. Freestone (eds.) International Law and Global Environmental Change, 21-39.

Garrick, J.A.F. and L.P. Schultz (1963) "A guide to the kinds of potentially dangerous sharks". In P.W.Gilbert, J.A.F. Garrick and L.P. Schultz (eds) <u>Sharks and Survival</u>. Boston : D.C. Heath and Company. pp.3-60.

Gaski, A.L. (1992) "<u>Sharks - species of special concern?</u>" Traffic USA, December.

Gilbert, C. and Gilbert, P.W. (1986) "The baffling basking shark", <u>Animal Kingdom</u>, 89 (3) 34-37.

Gilmore, R.G. (1980) " The Reproductive Biology of Lamnoid Sharks" In S.H. Gruber (ed) <u>Discovering Sharks,</u> Special Publication No.14 of the American Littoral Society, pages 64-67.

Goldman KJ, Anderson SD, McCosker JE and Klimley AP (1996) "Temperate, swimming depth, and movements of a white shark at the South Farallon Islands, California". *In:* <u>1993 Great White sharks. The biology of *Carcharodon carcharias*.</u> Klimley, AP & DP Ainley (eds) Academic Press, San Diego.

Gorman, T.B. and Dunstan, D.T. (1967) "Report on an attack by a great white shark off Coledale Beach, N.S.W., Australia, in which both the victim and attacker were recovered simultaneously", <u>California Fish and Game</u> 53, 219-23.

Grant, C.J., R.O. Sandland, and A.M. Olsen (1979) " Estimation of growth, mortality and yield per recruit of the Australian

School shark, *Galeorhinus australis* (Macleay), from tag recoveries" Australian Journal of Marine and Freshwater Research, 30, 625-37.

Gribble N (1996) Summary of the CITES discussion paper for the Animals Committee. In: Gribble, NA, G. McPherson & B. Lane (eds), Shark Management and Conservation: proceedings from the Sharks and Man workshop of the Second World Fish Congress Brisbane, Australia, 2 August 1996. Department of Primary Industries, Queensland.

Groombridge, B. (ed.) (1993) 1994 IUCN Red List of threatened animals. Cambridge, World Conservation Monitoring Centre.

Gruber, S.H. and C.A. Manire (1980) "The only good shark is a dead shark?" In S.H. Gruber (ed) Discovering Sharks, Special Publication No.14 of the American Littoral Society pages 115-121.

Hall, W.R. (1993) "Shark" MAS Bulletin, University of Delaware, Sea Grant College Program, 3 May 1993:1-6.

Hallacher, L.E. (1977) "On feeding behaviour of the basking shark, *Cetorhinus maximus*" Environmental Biology of Fishes, 2, 297-298.

Hamilton, W.J. III and K.E.F. Watt (1970) "Refuging" Annual Review of Ecology and Systematics 1, 263-86.

Hanchet, S (1988) "Reproductive biology of *Squalus acanthias* from the east coast, South Island, New Zealand". New Zealand Journal of Marine and Freshwater Research, 22 pp. 537-49.

Hancox, J (1994) "Harpoon hunter sails back into a storm", Sunday Telegraph, 18th September 1994.

Heist, E (1996) "Population genetics: an accessory to tagging studies", Shark News, Issue 7, June 1996: 4 -5.

Heuter, R.E. (1992) "Sportfishing tournaments for sharks in Florida, 1975-1990". Proceedings of the American Elasmobranch Society Annual Meeting, NewYork : 1991.

Hey, E (1993) "The precautionary principle", Marine Pollution Bulletin, 26, 53-54.

Hilton-Taylor, C. (compiler) (2000) 2000 IUCN Red List of Threatened Species. IUCN, Gland, Switzerland and Cambridge, UK.

Hoenig, J.M. and S.H. Gruber (1990) "Life history patterns in the elasmobranchs: implications for fisheries management". In H.L. Pratt Jr, S.H. Gruber and T. Taniuchi (eds) Elasmobranchs as living resources: advances in the biology, ecology, systematics and the status of the fisheries. NOAA Technical Report No. NMFS 90. Pp. 1-16

Hoff, T.B. (1990) "Conservation and management of the western North Atlantic shark resource based on the life history strategy limitations of the sandbar shark" Ph.D. Dissertation, University of Delaware, Newark.

Holden, M.J. (1974) "Problems in the rational exploitation of elasmobranch populations and some suggested solutions" In F. Harden Jones (ed.) Sea Fisheries Research, London: Logos, pp 187-215.

Holland, K.N., R.W. Brill and R.K.C. Chang (1990) "Horizontal and vertical movements of yellowfin and bigeye tuna associated with fish aggregating devices", US National Marine Fisheries Service Fishery Bulletin, 88, 493 -507.

Holland, K.N., C.G. Lowe, J.D. Peterson and A. Gill (1992) "Tracking coastal sharks with small boats: hammerhead shark pups as a case study" Aust. Journal of Marine and Freshwater Research, vol 43, no 1 pp61-66.

Holts, D.B. (1988) "Review of U.S. west coast commercial shark fisheries", US National Marine Fisheries Service Marine Fisheries Review 50 (1), 1-8.

Holts, D.B. and J. Sunada (1992) "California's pelagic shark fisheries". Proceedings of the American Elasmobranch Society Annual Meeting. New York : 1991.

Hubbell, G. (pers.comm.) Jaws International, 150 Buttonwood Drive, Key Biscayne, Florida 33149, USA. Tel. (305) 361-5890 Fax. (305) 361-5185

Huntsman, G.R. (1994) "Endangered marine finfish: Neglected resources or beast of fiction", Fisheries 19(7):8-15.

INEGI (1990) Estadisticas Historicas de Mexico. Volume II. Mexico. D.F.

Ito, R. and W. Machado. (1999). Annual report of the Hawaii-based longline fishery for 1998. NMFS Southwest Fisheries Science Center, Honolulu Laboratory Administrative Report. H-99-06.

Jenkins, S.H. (1988) "Use and abuse of demographic models of population growth" Bulletin, Ecological Society of America 69(4), 201-7.

Johnson, R.W. and D.R. Nelson (1973) "Agonistic display in the grey reef shark, *Carcharinus menisorrah,* and its relationship to man", Copeia, (1):76-84.

Joder, G. (1996) "Sharks: Ancient predators struggle for survival", Earth First!, Brigid 1996.

Jones, B.C. and Geen, G.H. (1977) "Reproduction and embryonic development of spiny dogfish (*Squalus acanthias*) in the Strait of Georgia, British Columbia". Journal of the Fisheries Research Board of Canada 34, 1286-92.

Kabasakal, H (1998) "Shark and ray fisheries in Turkey" Shark News 11, July 1998.

Kayama, M., Tsuchiya, Y. and Nevenzel, J.C. (1969) "The hydrocarbons of shark liver oils" Bulletin of the Japanese Society of Scientific Fisheries, 35, 653-664.

Ketchen, K.S. (1986) "The spiny dogfish (*Squalus acanthias*) in the northwest Pacific and a history of its utilization", Canadian Special Publication in Fisheries and Aquatic Science, 88:1-78.

Klimley, A.P. (1994) "The Predatory Behaviour of the White Shark", American Scientist, vol 82, no2:122-133.

Klimley, A.P. (1985) "Areal distribution and autecology of the white shark, *Carcharodon carcharias,* off the West coast of North America". South. Calif. Acad. Sci., Memoirs 9:15-40.

Klimley, A.P. (1980) "Observations of courtship and copulation in the nurse shark, *Ginglymostoma cirratum*", Copeia, No. 4:878-882.

Klimley AP and Anderson DS (1996) "Residency patterns of white sharks at the South Farrallon Islands, California". In: Great White Sharks: The biology of *Carcharodon carcharias*. AP Klimley & DG Ainley eds. Academic Press, New York USA Pp 365-373.

Klimley, A.P., S.B. Butler, D.R. Nelson and A.T. Stull (1988) "Diel movements of scalloped hammerhead sharks, *Sphyrna lewini* Griffith and Smith, to and from a seamount in the Gulf of California",Journal of Fish Biology 33, 751-61.

Klimley, A.P. and D.R. Nelson (1984) "Diel movement patterns of the scalloped hammerhead shark (*Sphyrna lewini*) in relation to El Bajo Espiritu Santo: a refuging central-position social system" Behavioural Ecology and Sociobiology 15, 45-54.

Kornfield, I., B.D. Sidell and P.S. Gagnon (1982) "Stock definition in Atlantic herring (*Clupea harengus harengus*): genetic evidence for discrete fall and spring populations" Canadian Journal of Fisheries and Aquatic Sciences, 39, 1610-1621.

Kunzlik, P.A. (1988) "The basking shark" Scottish Fisheries Information Pamphlet, 14, 21pp Aberdeen.

Last PR and Stevens JD (1994) Sharks and Rays of Australia CSIRO Division of Fisheries, Australia.

LeBoeuf, B.J., M. Riedman and R.S. Keys (1982) "White shark predation on pinnipeds in California coastal waters". Fish. Bull. NOAA/NMFS, 80(4):891-4.

Lenanton, R.C.J., D.I. Heald, M. Platell, M. Cliff and J. Shaw (1990) "Aspects of the Reproductive Biology of the Gummy Shark, *Mustelus antarcticus* Gunther, from Waters off the South Coast of Western Australia", Aust. J. Mar. Freshwater Res., 41:807-22.

Lien, J and Fawcett, L (1986) "Distribution of basking sharks, *Cetorhinus maximus,* incidentally caught in inshore fishing gear in Newfoundland" Canadian Field-Naturalist, 100, 246-252.

MAFF Statistics (pers comm.) Matthew Elliott, MAFF Fisheries Statistics Unit, 0207-238-6697

Manire, C and S. Gruber (1990) "Many sharks may be headed toward extinction", Conservation Biology, 4 (1):10-11.

Marine Conservation Society (pers. comm.) Sam Pollard, 01989-566017.

Marr, J.C. (1951) "On the use of the terms abundance, availability and apparent abundance in fishery biology", Copeia, 163-169.

Matthews, L.H. (1950) "Reproduction in the basking shark, *Cetorhinus maximus*", Philos.Trans.Zool.Soc.Lond.(B), 234:247-316.

Matthews, L.H. and H.W. Parker (1950) "Notes on the anatomy and biology of the basking shark (*Cetorhinus maximum* (Gunner))", Proc.Zool.Soc.Lond., 120:535-76.

Matthiessen, P. (1971) Blue Meridian : The Search for the Great White Shark. New York: Random House.

Maxwell, G. (1952) Harpoon at a Venture, London: Rupert Hart-Davies, 272pp.

McCormick, H.W., Allen, T and Young W.E. (1964) Shadows in the Sea. London: Sidgwick and Jackson, 415pp.

McGregor, C. (1988) "The southern shark fishery: a plan to safeguard the resource" Australian Fisheries 47(4), 2-7.

McKibben, J.N. and D.R. Nelson (1986) "Patterns of movement and grouping of gray reef sharks, *Carcharhinus amblyrhynchos*, at Enewetak, Marshall Islands"<u>Bulletin of Marine Science</u> 38(1), 89-110.

McNally, K (1976) <u>The sun-fish hunt</u>. Belfast, Blackstaff Press Ltd., 80pp.

Marashi SH (1996) <u>Summary Information on the Role of International Fishery and Other Bodies with Regard to the Conservation and Management of Living Resources of the High Seas</u>. FAO Fisheries Circular No.908 (United Nations Food and Agriculture Organisation, Rome) 104 pages

Miller, D.J. and R.S. Collier (1981) "Shark attacks in California and Oregon, 1926-1979". <u>Calif.Fish Game,</u> 67(2):76-104.

Mitchell, R (1991) "Sharks in Danger", <u>World of Fishing</u>, p81-82.

Moreno J.A. and J. Moron (1992) "Reproductive biology of the bigeye thresher shark, *Alopias superciliosus* (Lowe,1839)"<u>Aust.Journal of Marine and Freshwater Research</u> vol 43, no 1 pp 77-86.

Morrissey, J.F. and S.H. Gruber (1989) "So excellent a fish" <u>Earthwatch</u> October, 1989:16-21.

Mundus, F. and B. Wisner (1971) <u>Sport fishing for sharks</u>. New York : Macmillan, 380 p.

Musick, J.A. (1996) "Critically endangered large coastal sharks, a case study: the sandbar shark *Carcharhinus plumbeus* (Nardo, 1827)", <u>Shark News</u> (Newsletter of the IUCN Shark Specialist Group).

Musick, J.A., S. Branstetter and J.A. Colvocoresses (1992) "Analysis of shark catches for 1974-1990 for the Chesapeake Bight Region of the U.S. Mid-Atlantic coast". <u>Proceedings of the American Elasmobranch Society Annual Meeting,</u> New York. 1991.

Myklevoll, S. (1968) "Basking shark fishery", <u>Commercial Fisheries Review,</u> July, 59-63.

Nakano, H., and K. Nakaya (1987) "Records of the White Shark *Carcharodon carcharias* from Hokkaido, Japan". <u>Japanese Journal of Ichthyology</u> 33(4): 414-16.

Nakaya, K. (1994) "Distribution of white shark in Japanese waters", <u>Fisheries Science,</u> 60 (5), 515-518.

Nédéléc .C & Prado J (1990) <u>Definition and Classification of fishing gear categories</u>. FAO Fisheries Technical Paper No. 222, Rev. 1. FAO, Rome, Italy 92 pages

Norman, J.R. and F.C. Fraser (1937) Giant fishes, whales and dolphins. New York : W.W. Norton.

Nuttall, N. (1996) "Expert claims cover-up on Med's great white sharks", The Times, 25 July, 1996.

Oliver A (1996) "Draft Discussion Paper Pursuant to CITES Resolution Conf. 9.17: An Overview of the Biological Status of Shark Species". 15 July 1996. National Marine Fisheries Service, Silver Spring, Maryland.

Olsen, A.M. (1954) "The biology, migration and growth rate of the school shark, *Galeorhinus australis* (Macleay) (Carcharhinidae) in south-eastern Australian waters". Australian Journal of Marine and Freshwater Research, 5, 353-410.

Olsen, A.M. (1984) "Synopsis of biological data on the school shark, *Galeorhinus australis* (Macleay, 1881). FAO Fisheries Synopsis No. 139.

Otway, NM and Parker PC (1999) "A review of the biology and ecology of the grey nurse shark *(Carcharias taurus)* Rafinesque 1810. NSW Fisheries Research Report Series 1. NSW Fisheries.

Palacio, F.J. (1995) <u>Report to the CITES Secretariat on participation in the 21st session of the FAO Committee on fisheries to present CITES Resolution Conf. 9.17 on "Status of International Trade in Shark Species", and overview of pertinent activities,</u> Panama: Working Group on Sharks.

Parker, H.W. and M. Boeseman (1954) "The basking shark, *Cetorhinus maximus* in winter", <u>Proc.Zool.Soc.Lond.</u>, 124(1):185-94.

Parker, H.W. and F.C. Stott (1965) "Age, size and vertebral Calcification in the basking shark, *Cetorhinus maximum* (Gunnerus)", <u>Zool. Meded.</u>, 40(34):305-19.

Parry-Jones R (1996) TRAFFIC report on shark fisheries and trade in Hong Kong In: Phipps MJ (Comp) <u>TRAFFIC [East Asia] report on shark fisheries and trade in the East Asian region</u> TRAFFIC East Asia – Taipei.

Paterson, R.A. (1986) "Shark prevention measures working well", <u>Australian Fisheries</u> March, 12-18.

Paterson, R.A. (1990) "Effects of long-term anti-shark measures on target and non -target species in Queensland, Australia",<u>Biological Conservation,</u> 52:147-159.

Pepperell, J (1992) "Trends in the distribution, species composition and size of sharks caught by gamefish anglers off south-eastern

Australia, 1961-1990" <u>Australian Journal of Marine and Freshwater Research,</u> 43 (1), 213-25.

Perrine, D. (1995) <u>Sharks.</u> Grantown-on-Spey, Scotland : Colin Baxter Photography Ltd.

Pike, C.S. III (1980) "Uncovering the ages of sharks and its importance in fisheries management" In S.H. Gruber (ed) <u>Discovering Sharks,</u> Special Publication No.14 of the American Littoral Society pages 109-111.

Pollard DA, Lincoln Smith MP and Smith AK (1996) "The biology and conservation status of the grey nurse shark *(Carcharias taurus* Rafinesque 1810) in New South Wales, Australia". <u>Aquatic Conservation: Marine and Freshwater Ecosystems</u> 1:177.1-20

Pough, F.H., J.B. Heiser and W.N. McFarland (1989) <u>Vertebrate Life</u> London : Collier Macmillan Publishers.

Pratt, H.L. Jr. (1996) "Reproduction in the male white shark (*Carcharodon carcharias*)". In A.P. Klimley & D.G. Ainley (eds) <u>Great White Sharks : Ecology and Behaviour</u> : Orlando, Academic Press.

Pratt, H.L., Jr., J.G. Casey and R.B. Conklin (1982) "Observations on large white sharks, *Carcharodon carcharias,* off Long Island, New York". <u>Fish.Bull.NOAA/NMFS,</u> 80(1):153-7.

Pratt, H.L. and T. Otake (1990) 'Recommendations for work needed to increase our knowledge of reproduction relative to fishery management' In H.L. Pratt, Jr., S.H. Gruber and T. Taniuchi (eds) <u>Elasmobranchs as living resources: advances in the biology, ecology, systematics and the status of fisheries</u> : US Department of Commerce, NOAA Technical Report NMFS 90, pp. 509-510.

Pratt, H.L. and J.C. Carrier (1995) "Wild mating of the Nurse Sharks", <u>National Geographic</u>, vol.187, no.5, May 1995 page 44-53.

Presser, J., & R. Allen (1995) "Management of the white shark in South Australia". <u>SA Fisheries Management Series, Paper 6, May 1995.</u> Primary Industries, South Australian Dept. Fisheries (PISA), Adelaide, 18 pp.

Pyle, P (1992) "Sympathy for a predator" <u>Quarterly Review of the Point Reyes Bird Observatory,</u> Number 93, spring/summer 1992.

Randall, J.E. (1973) "Size of the Great white shark *(Carcharodon)*", <u>Science, Wash.,</u> 181(4095): 169-70.

Randall, J.E. (1992) "Review of the biology of the tiger shark (*Galeocerdo cuvier*)" <u>Aust. Journal of Marine and Freshwater Research,</u> vol 43, no 1 pp21-31.

Reid, D.D. and M. Krogh (1992) "Assessment of catches from protective shark meshing off New South Wales beaches between 1950 and 1990" Australian Journal of Marine and Freshwater Research, Vol 43, No 1 pp 283-96.

Richard, J (1994) "Shark Survival: is management too late?" Sport Fishing February 1994: 58-64.

Richards, J.B. (1987) "Developing a localized fishery: the Pacific angel shark" In S. Cook (ed) Sharks: an inquiry into biology, behavior, fisheries and use, Oregon State University Sea Grant Publication, Corvallis, Oregon:147-160.

Ripley, W.E. (1946) "The soupfin shark and the fishery" Fish Bulletin (California), 64, 7-37.

Roedel, P.M. and Ripley, W.E. (1950) "California sharks and rays", Fish Bulletin (California), 75, 88pp.

Rose, D.A. (1991) "A North American Free Trade Agreement: The Impacts on Wildlife Trade". World Wildlife Fund.

Rose, D. (1996) "Social and economic importance of elasmobranchs" chapter to the Global Shark Action Plan of the IUCN Shark Specialist Group.

Rose. D (1996) "An Overview of World Trade in Sharks and Other Cartilaginous Fishes" TRAFFIC Network 106pp

Rose. D (1998) "Shark Fisheries and Trade in the Americas, Volume 1: North America" TRAFFIC TRAFFIC North America 142pp

Rose-Hopkins, D (1992) "The sharks of Mexico: a resource for all seasons" TRAFFIC USA, Dec. 1992 pp 4-6.

Russell, D (1996) " Sharks: hunters hunted", Salt Water Sportsman, March 1996:60 110.

Salini, J.P., S.J.M. Blaber and D.T. Brewer (1992) "Diets of sharks from estuaries and adjacent waters of the north-eastern Gulf of Carpentaria, Australia". Aust.J.Mar.Freshwater Res. 43:87-96.

Sant G & Hayes E (eds) (1996) "The Oceania Region's Harvest, Trade and Management of Sharks and other Cartilaginous Fish: An Overview" TRAFFIC Oceania 70pp

Scott, GP (1996) "Updated analysis of recent trends in catch rates of some Atlantic sharks". 1996 NMFS Stock Evaluation Workshop document SB-III-17 NMFS Southeast Fish. Sci. Center, Miami FL.

Scott, G, Phares PJ & Slater B (1996) "Recreational catch, average size and effort information for shark in US Atlantic and Gulf of

Mexico waters". 1996 NMFS Stock Evaluation Workshop document SB-III-5. NMFS Southeast Fish. Sci. Center, Miami FL.

Scott, M (2000) "Save our Sharks". South China Morning Post 20 July 2000.

Siccardi, E.M. (1960) "*Cetorhinus* in el Atlantico sur". Actas y trabajos del Primer Congreso Sudamericano de Zoologia, La Plata, 1959, vol. 4:251-63.

Siccardi, E.M. (1961) "*Cetorhinus* en el Atlantico sur" (Elasmobranchii: Cetorhinidae). Rev. Mus. Argent. Cienc. Nat. Bernardino Rivadavia Inst. Nac. Invest. Cienc. Nat., 6(2):61-101.

Simpfendorfer, C.A. (1991) "The Queensland shark meshing program: analysis of the results from Townsville, North Queensland", Proceedings of Conservation Workshop, Sharks Down Under Conference, Sydney.

Simpfendorfer, C.A. (1992) "*Reproductive* strategy of the Australian sharpnose shark, *Rhizoprionodon taylori* (Elasmobranchii:Carcharhinidae), from Cleveland Bay, northern Queensland", Aust.J.of Marine and Freshwater Research vol 43, no 1 pp 67-75.

Simpfendorfer, C.A. (1992) "Biology of tiger sharks (*Galeocerdo cuvier*) caught by the Queensland Shark Meshing Program off Townsville, Australia" <u>Aust. Journal of Marine and Freshwater Research</u>, vol 43, no 1 pp 33-43.

Simpfendorfer, C.A. (1993) "Age and growth of the Australian Sharpnose shark, *Rhizoprionodon taylori,* from north Queensland, Australia", <u>Environmental Biology of Fishes,</u> 36:233-241.

Simpfendorfer, C.A. and N.E. Milward (1993) "Utilisation of a tropical bay as a nursery area by sharks of the families Carcharhinidae and Sphyrnidae", <u>Environmental Biology of Fishes,</u> 37:337-345.

Skomal, G. and B. Chase (1996) "Release mortality studies in Massachusetts" <u>Shark News</u> Issue 7, June 1996: 8-9.

Sminkey, T.R. and J.A. Musick (1996) "Demographic analysis of sandbar sharks in the western North Atlantic", <u>Fishery Bulletin.</u>

Smith, S.E. and Abramson, N.J. (1990) "Leopard shark *Triakis semifasciata* distribution, mortality rate, yield, and stock replenishment estimates based on a tagging study in San

Francisco Bay" <u>US National Marine Fisheries Service Fishery Bulletin</u> 88, 371-81.

Smith, P.J., R.I.C.C. Francis and M. McVeagh (1991) "Loss of genetic diversity due to fishing pressure", <u>Fisheries Research,</u> 10, 309-316.

Snelson, F.F., T.J. Mulligan & S.E. Williams (1984) "Food habits, occurrence and population structure of the bull shark, *Carcharinus leucas* in Florida coastal lagoons" <u>Bull. Mar. Sci.</u> 34:71-80.

Springer, S. (1939) "The great white shark, *Carcharodon carcharias* (Linnaeus) in Florida waters".<u>Copeia</u> 1939 : 114-115.

Springer, S. (1967) "Social organisation of shark populations" In P.W. Gilbert, R.F. Mathewson & D.P.Rall (eds.) <u>Sharks, Skates and Rays,</u> John Hopkins University Press, Baltimore, pp 149-174.

Springer, S . and P.W. Gilbert (1976) "The basking shark, *Cetorhinus maximus,* from Florida and California, with comments on its biology and systematics". <u>Copeia,</u> 1963(2):245-51.

Squire, J.L., Jr. (1967) "Observations of basking sharks and great white sharks in Monterey Bay", <u>Copeia,</u> 1967(1):247-50.

Squire, J.L., Jr. (1990) "Distribution and apparent abundance of the basking shark, *Cetorhinus maximus*, off the central and southern Californian Coast, 1962-85"Mar.Fish.Rev., vol 52, no.2, pp 8-11.

Stead, D.G. (1963) Sharks and Rays of Australian seas. Sydney : Angus and Robertson, 211 p.

Stevens, J.D. (1984) "Biological observations on sharks caught by sport fishermen off New South Wales" Australian Journal of Marine and Freshwater Research 35, 573-90.

Stevens, J.D. (1987) Sharks. London : Merehurst Press.

Stevens, J.D. (1992) "Blue and mako shark by-catch in the Japanese longline fishery off south-eastern Australia" Aust. Journal of Marine and Freshwater Research, vol 43, no 1 pp227-36.

Stevens, J.D. and McLoughlin, K.J. (1991) "Distribution, size and sex composition, reproductive biology and diet of sharks from northern Australia" Australian Journal of Marine and Freshwater Research, 42, 151-99.

Stevens, J.D. and P.D. Wiley (1986) "Biology of Two Commercially Important Carcharhinid Sharks from Northern Australia", Aust. J. Mar. Freshw. Res., 37:671-88.

Stewart, B.S. and P.K. Yochem (1985) "Radio-Tagged Harbor Seal *Phoca citulina richardsi,* eaten by White Shark, *Carcharodon carcharias*, in the Southern California Bight". <u>California Fish and Game</u> 71(2):113-15.

Stoessell, T (1992) "Shark fin trade booms", <u>Traffic</u>, December 1992.

Stott, F.C. (1982) "A note on catches of basking sharks, *Cetorhinus maximus* (Gunnerus), off Norway and their relation to possible migration paths", <u>J.Fish.Biol,</u> vol 21, no.2:227-230.

Strasberg, D.W. (1958) "Distribution, abundance, and habits or pelagic sharks in the central Pacific Ocean", <u>Fish. Bull. U.S. Fish. Wildl. Serv.,</u> 58:335-61.

Strong, W.R. Jr., B.D. Bruce, R.C. Murphy & D. R. Nelson (1996) "Patterns of movement, distribution and abundance of great white sharks *Carcharodon carcharias* in South Australian waters" In A.P. Klimley & D.G. Ainley (eds) <u>Great White Sharks : Ecology and Behaviour</u> : Orlando, Academic Press.

Strong, W.R. Jr., R.C. Murphy, B.D. Bruce and D.R. Nelson (1992) " Movements and associated observations of bait-attracted white sharks, *Carcharodon carcharias* : a preliminary report" <u>Aust. Journal of Marine and Freshwater Research</u>, vol 43, no 1 pp13-20.

Sund, O (1943) "Et brugdebarsel", <u>Naturen,</u> 67, 285-286.

Swaby, S.E. and G.W. Potts (1990) "Rare British marine fishes - identification and conservation", Journal of Fish Biology, 37, Supplement A, 133-143.

Thorson, T.B. (1982) "The impact of commercial exploitation on Sawfish and shark populations in Lake Nicaragua", Fisheries, vol 7, no 2 : 2-10.

TRAFFIC (1995) "A TRAFFIC Network Report to the CITES Animals Committee on the TRAFFIC Network Global Shark Trade Study" TRAFFIC OCEANIA & TRAFFIC USA, August 1995 3pp

TRAFFIC (2000) "Sustainable use of large migratory fish in the Southern and Indian Oceans: Gaps in the International Legal Framework" TRAFFIC Website www.traffic.org/migratoryfish

Tricas, T.C. and E.M.Le Feuvre (1985) "Mating in the reef white-tip shark *Triaenodon obesus*", Marine Biology 84:233-237.

Trono, R. (1996) "Philippine whale shark and manta ray fisheries", Shark News, Issue 7, June 1996:13.

Tsamenyi M & Woodhill F (2000) "Sustainable Use of Large Migratory Fish in the Southern and Indian Oceans: Gaps in the International Legal Framework" TRAFFIC.

Uchida, S., M. Toda, K. Teshima and K. Yano (1995). "Pregnant white shark and full-term embryos from Japan" In A.P. Klimley & D.G. Ainley (eds) Great White Sharks : Ecology and Behaviour: Orlando, Academic Press.

Van Deinse, A.B. and M.J. Adriani (1953) "On the absence of gillrakers in specimens of the basking shark, *Cetorhinus maximus* (Gunner)", Zool. Meded., 31:307-10.

Vas, P. (1990) "The abundance of the blue shark, *Prionace glauca*, in the western English Channel", Environmental Biology of Fishes, 29, 209-225.

Vas, P. (1991) "A field guide to the sharks of British coastal waters", Field Studies, 7, 651-686.

Vas, P. (1994) "Recreational catches of blue shark (*Prionace glauca*) in the western English Channel 1984-93" in S.L. Fowler and R.C. Earll (eds) (1994) Proceedings of Second European Shark and Ray Workshop, 15-16 February 1994. Tag and Release Schemes and Shark and Ray Management Plans. Marine Branch, Joint Nature Conservation Committee, Monkstone House, Peterborough, UK.

Vas, P. (1995) "The status and conservation of sharks in Britain", Aquatic Conservation: Marine and Freshwater Ecosystems, Vol. 5, 67-79.

Walker, T.I. (1992) "Fishery simulation model for sharks applied to the gummy shark, *Mustelus antarcticus* Gunther, from southern Australian waters" Aust. Journal of Marine and Freshwater Research, vol 43, no 1 pp195-212.

Walker, T. (1996) "Localised stock depletion: does it occur for sharks?" Shark News Issue 6, March 1996: 1-2.

Walker T, Johnson D, Brown D, and McLoughlin K (1997) The Southern Shark Fishery 1997, Fisheries Assessment Report.

Watkins, A (1958) The sea my hunting ground. London, Heinemann 250 pp.

Weber, M.L & Fordham (1997) "Managing Shark Fisheries: Opportunities for International Conservation" TRAFFIC International and the Center for Marine Conservation 61pp

Williams, T. (1995) "Why marine fish management hasn't worked" Fly Rod and Reel, January/ February 1995:13-17.

Williams, H and A.H. Schaap (1992) "Preliminary results of a study into the incidental mortality of sharks in gill-nets in two

Tasmanian shark nursery areas" Aust. Journal of Marine and Freshwater Research, vol 43, no 1 pp237-50.

Witner SP and Cliff G (1998) "Age and growth determination of the white shark, *Carcharodon carcharias,* from the east coast of South Africa". Fish Bulletin 97(1): 153-169.

Wood, C.C., Ketchen, K.S., Beamish, R.J. (1979) "Population dynamics of spiny dogfish (*Squalus acanthias*) in British Columbia waters" Journal of the Fisheries Research Board of Canada, 36, 647-56.

Young, J.Z. (1962) The Life of Vertebrates. Oxford, Oxford University Press.

ACKNOWLEDGEMENTS

I would like to thank Mike Pawson and Martin Speight for their kind supervision and advice. Thanks must also be extended to Sam Pollard at the Marine Conservation Society, Sarah Fowler at The Shark Trust, Nick Dulvy, Caroline Pollock at the IUCN, Artur Payer and Palacios Alberti at EC Fisheries, Simon Waterfield at MAFF, John Angel at the DETR, Fernandez Galiano at the Council of Europe, Strasbourg, Robert Vagg at UNEP, Paul Knapman at English Nature, Alison Bailey and Rebecca Evans at the Institute of Biology, and Matthew Elliott at MAFF Statistics. Special thanks to Rodney, Andrew and Silvy Fox for use of their slides for the cover page of this book and to Julian Cunningham-Day for his patience and support.

APPENDICES

Appendix 1 Legislation that protects white sharks or identifies their status as needing particular conservation action in Australia

Commonwealth

Endangered Species Protection Act 1992 **S.25 Schedule 1 Part 2.**

Vulnerable

17 December 1997

replaced by the

Environment Protection and Biodiversity Conservation Act 1999 **Part 13** *Vulnerable*

17 July 2000

Southern Australia

Fisheries Act 1982 **S.42**

A person must not take a fish declared by regulation to be protected

1 January 1998

Victoria

Fisheries Act 1995 **S.71**

A person must not take, injure, damage, destroy, possess, keep, display for reward, release or sell any protected biota

4 August 1998

Tasmania

Living Marine Resources Management Act 1995 **S.135(2)**

A person must not take any protected fish.

New South Wales

Fisheries Management Act 1994

Part 7a Protected Species under Schedule 5 (Species vulnerable to extinction)

S.8 Fisheries Closure Notification - taking of white sharks prohibited by all methods in all waters except

approved shark meshing contractors for scientific purposes.

Protected under Section 7a on 14 May 1999 Gazetted January 1997 Section 8.

Western Australia

Fisheries Resources Management Act 1994 **S.46**

A person must not take, possess, sell or purchase, consign, bring into the state any totally protected fish

November 1997

Queensland

Fisheries Act 1994 **S.78 (1)**

A person must not unlawfully take, possess or sell a regulated fish

18 July 1997

Compiled by CSIRO Marine Research

Appendix 2 Australia's Draft Grey Nurse Shark Recovery Plan

Recovery Objectives

The overall recovery objective is:

To promote the recovery of grey nurse shark numbers in Australian waters to a level that will see the species removed from the schedules of the ESP Act.

The specific objectives are to:

A. Reduce the impact of commercial fishing on grey nurse sharks.

B. Reduce the impact of recreational fishing on grey nurse sharks.

C. Reduce the impact of shark control activities on grey nurse sharks.

D. Identify and establish refugia to protect grey nurse sharks from threatening activities such as commercial and recreational fishing at key locations.

E. Reduce the impact of shark finning on grey nurse sharks.

F. Develop research programs towards conservation of grey nurse sharks.

G. Develop population models to assess populations and monitor recovery.

H. Manage the impact of ecotourism on grey nurse sharks.

I. Reduce the impact of aquaria on grey nurse sharks.

J. Promote community education.

K. Reassess the conservation status of the grey nurse shark.

The recovery of grey nurse sharks will take time. The need to make informed decisions based on the best available information is also acknowledged as a principal activity of this plan.

Actions and Recovery Criteria

To fulfil the specific objectives of this plan, actions are designed to identify and reduce the threats to grey nurse sharks, determine levels of mortality and reduce that mortality. The assessment of the actions against the criteria for success is essential to measure the recovery of grey nurse sharks. These actions and criteria are summarised as:

• assess commercial and recreational fisheries data to determine current level of grey nurse by-catch;

• modify fisheries logbooks to record grey nurse catch and biological data;

• ensure existing fishery observer programs record interactions with grey nurse shark;

• quantify and reduce levels of grey nurse take in shark control activities;

- establish community based programs to identify and monitor key sites for grey nurse sharks;
- develop appropriate mechanisms to protect key sites;
- establish tag and release programs;
- prevent unregulated shark finning;
- assess the population size and status of grey nurse sharks;
- collect biological and genetic information;
- minimise ecotourism and aquaria impact on grey nurse sharks;
- develop a community education strategy for grey nurse sharks; and
- reassessment of the conservation status of grey nurse shark.

Evaluation and Review

The life of the plan is 5 years. The ESP Act states the need to evaluate the performance of the plan. A review will be carried out annually by the recovery team. The recovery team will also undertake an evaluation of the plan after 5 years.

Appendix 3 Australia's Draft Great White Shark Recovery Plan

Recovery Objectives

The overall recovery objective is:

To recover white shark numbers in Australian waters, to a level that will see the species removed from the schedules of the ESP Act (based on the IUCN (1994) criteria).

The specific objectives are to:

A. Reduce the impact of commercial fishing on white sharks.

B. Investigate and evaluate the impact of recreational fishing on white sharks.

C. Monitor and reduce the impact of shark control activities on white sharks.

D. Reduce the impact of trade in white shark products.

E. Manage the impact of ecotourism on white sharks.

F. Develop research programs towards the conservation of white sharks.

G. Identify and establish refugia to protect and conserve white sharks

H. Promote community education.

Actions and Recovery Criteria

To fulfil the specific objectives, actions are designed to identify and reduce the threats to white sharks, determine levels of mortality and reduce that mortality. The assessment of the actions against the criteria for success is essential for the successful recovery of white sharks identified in this plan. These actions and criteria can be found in Table 4 and are summarised as:

Prescribed Action

- assess available commercial and recreational fisheries data to determine current level of white shark by-catch;
- modify commercial fisheries logbooks to record white shark catch and biological data;
- ensure existing fishery observer programs record interactions with white sharks;
- quantify and reduce levels of white shark take in shark control activities;
- establish tag and release programs in shark control and research programs;
- regulate shark finning;
- model population and status of white sharks;
- collect biological and genetic information;

- minimise ecotourism impact on white sharks; and

- develop a community education strategy for white sharks.

Evaluation and Review

The life of the plan is 5 years. The ESP Act states the need to evaluate the performance of the plan. A review will be carried out annually by the recovery team. The recovery team will also undertake an evaluation of the plan after 5 years.

Appendix 4 Draft discussion paper persuant to CITES Resolution Conf. 9.17 (1996f:22-23)

Recommends research and management efforts to address the following:

1. expand efforts to collect information on the life-history and biological parameters such as growth rate, life span, sexual maturity, fecundity and stock-recruitment relationships of sharks taken in directed fisheries or as by-catch

2. develop species-specific baseline information about shark populations and fisheries

3. document the distribution of sharks by age, sex and seasonal movements

4. identify the location of shark nursery habitats and determine their ecological parameters such as the presence and abundance of prey, competition with other species, predators of young, basic water chemistry, possible pollutants and competition with man for food and species (Pratt and Otake, 1990:509-510)

5. document the extent of losses and/or degradation of nursery habitats and the effect on shark populations

6. determine the relationship between shark populations and overexploitation of prey species

7. improve fisheries statistics on sharks to reflect total fishing pressure on a species basis including directed commercial and recreational fisheries and by-catch

8. mechanisms should be explored to evaluate the survival of sharks discarded alive

9. discourage finning and wilful by-catch mortality. Encourage live release, tagging and tag reporting by commercial fishermen (Fowler and Earll, 1994)

10. steps should be taken to develop criteria for discriminating between shark species after carcasses have been dressed

11. conduct experimental investigations of shark population response to different types of management measures

12. cooperate in the development of regional programmes specifically dedicated to coordinating data collection and information sharing to provide accurate stock assessments of shared shark species

13. given the time required to organize, fund and collect the information necessary to accurately ascertain the biological status of sharks, adopt a conservative or precautionary

approach towards the harvest of shark species in order to ensure sustainable utilisation.

Appendix 5 Aims of a National Shark-Plan, as set out in the FAO International Plan of Action for Sharks

1. Ensure that shark catches from directed and non-directed fisheries are sustainable

2. Assess threats to shark populations, determine and protect critical habitats and implement harvesting strategies consistent with the principles of biological sustainability and rational long-term economic use

3. Identify and pay special attention, in particular, to vulnerable or threatened species

4. Improve and develop frameworks for establishing and coordinating effective consultation involving all stakeholders in research, management and educational initiatives within and between States

5. Minimise unutilised incidental catches of sharks

6. Contribute to the protection of biodiversity and ecosystem structure and function

7. Minimise waste and discards from shark fisheries in accordance with paragraph 7.2.2g of the Code of Conduct for

Responsible Fisheries (e.g. requiring the retention of the sharks from which fins are removed)

8. Encourage full use of dead sharks

9. Facilitate improved species-specific catch and landings data and monitoring of shark fisheries

10. Facilitate the identification and reporting of species-specific biological and trade data

Appendix 6 IUCN Guidelines for Protected Area Management

Category Ia

Strict Nature Reserve : Protected Area managed mainly for science

Area of land and/or sea possessing some outstanding or representative ecosystems, geological or physiological features and/or species, available primarily for scientific research and/or environmental monitoring.

Category Ib

Wilderness Area: Protected Area managed mainly for wilderness protection

Large area of unmodified or slightly modified land and/or sea, retaining its natural character and influence, without permanent or significant habitation, which is protected and managed so as to preserve its natural condition.

Category II

National Park: Protected Area managed mainly for ecosystem conservation and recreation

Natural area of land and/or sea, designated to (a) protect the ecological integrity of one or more ecosystems for this and future generations, (b) exclude exploitation or occupation inimical to the purposes of designation of the area and (c) provide a foundation for spiritual, scientific, educational, recreational and visitor opportunities, all of which must be environmentally and culturally compatible.

Category III

Natural Monument: Protected Area managed for conservation of specific natural features

Area containing one or more specific natural or natural/cultural features which is of outstanding value because of its inherent rarity, representative or aesthetic qualities or cultural significance.

Category IV

Habitat/Species Management Area: Protected Area managed mainly for conservation through

management intervention

Area of land and/or sea subject to active intervention for management purposes so as to ensure the maintenance of habitats and/or to meet the requirements of specific species.

Category V

Protected Landscape/Seascape: Protected Areas managed mainly for landscape/seascape conservation and recreation

Area of land, with coast and seas as appropriate, where the interaction of people and nature over time has produced an area of distinct character with significant aesthetic, cultural and/or ecological value, and often with high biological diversity. Safeguarding the integrity of this traditional interaction is vital to the protection, maintenance and evolution of such an area.

Category VI

Managed Resource Protected Areas: Protected Area managed mainly for the sustainable use of natural ecosystems

Area containing predominantly unmodified natural systems, managed to ensure long term protection and maintenance of biological diversity, while providing at the same time a sustainable flow of natural products and services to meet community needs.

(Anon1994f)

Appendix 7 Goals of the National Representative System of Marine Protected Areas in Australia

The primary goal of the NRSMPA is to establish and manage a comprehensive, adequate and representative system of MPAs to contribute to the long-term ecological viability of marine and estuarine systems, and to protect Australia's biological diversity at all levels.

The following secondary goals are designed to be compatible with the primary goal:

- To promote the development of MPAs within the framework of integrated ecosystem management;
- To provide a formal management framework for a broad spectrum of human activities, including recreation, tourism, shipping and the use or extraction of resources, the impacts of which are compatible with the primary goal;
- To provide scientific reference sites;
- To provide for the special needs of rare, threatened or depleted species and threatened ecological communities;
- To provide for the conservation of special groups of organisms, e.g. species with complex habitat requirements or mobile or migratory

species, or species vulnerable to disturbance which may depend on reservation for their conservation;

• To protect areas of high conservation value including those containing high species diversity, natural refugia for flora and fauna and centres of endemism;

• To provide for the recreational, aesthetic and cultural needs of indigenous and non-indigenous people.

(ANZECC 1998)